O9-AIF-344

salads:
beyond the bowl

MINDY FOX

salads: beyond the bowl

EXTRAORDINARY RECIPES FOR EVERYDAY EATING

PHOTOGRAPHY BY ELLEN SILVERMAN
KYLE BOOKS

Published in 2012 by Kyle Books
www.kylebooks.com

Distributed by National Book Network
4501 Forbes Blvd., Suite 200
Lanham, MD 20706
Phone: (800) 462-6420
Fax: (301) 429-5746
custserv@nbnbooks.com

ISBN: 978-1-906868-67-3

All rights reserved. No reproduction,
copy or transmission of this publication
may be made without written permission.
No paragraph of this publication may be
reproduced, copied or transmitted save
with the written permission or in accordance
with the provision of the Copyright Act
1956 (as amended). Any person who does
any unauthorized act in relation to this
publication may be liable to criminal
prosecution and civil claims for damages.

Text © 2012 by Mindy Fox
Photographs © 2012 by Ellen Silverman
Book design © 2012 by Kyle Books

Project editor Anja Schmidt
Designer Carl Hodson
Photographer Ellen Silverman
Food styling Rebecca Jurkevich
Prop styling Lucy Attwater
Copy editor Sarah Scheffel
Production Gemma John and Nic Jones

Library of Congress Control Number:
2011945813

Color reproduction by Scanhouse
Printed and bound in China by Toppan Leefung

introduction

I have always loved salad. My understanding of exactly what a "salad" is, though, has dramatically evolved as my life has progressed.

I grew up in the 1970s and spent the better part of my pre-teen years in the Chicago-area suburbs. It was the dawn of the gourmet grocer, but most people still shopped at the regular supermarket, where the lettuce section consisted of orbs of iceberg and the random head of romaine—nothing like the luxe lineup of lettuce and salad green varieties we enjoy today.

My mom was brilliant in the kitchen—an original food enthusiast. She showed my brother Jason and I how to fry Chinese shrimp chips, lovingly lacquer spareribs with homemade barbeque sauce and pinch back basil leaves from her small backyard herb patch, opening our eyes to the magic of kitchen alchemy and garden-to-table eating. Still, in keeping with the times, her vegetables during those years were purchased at the A&P, and mostly they were cooked on the stovetop or in the fondue pot.

The raw vegetables I encountered in my early life were on the crudité plate at my grandmother's beach house. Nanny never missed her ritual five o'clock vodka, and with it she offered a glass platter of perfectly chilled, impossibly crisp veggies: crunchy radishes, those peppery and pretty red baubles with icy white insides that excited my taste buds; cucumber spears, their thick skins peeled away but sweet popping seeds left intact; freshly sliced celery with pleasingly bitter juices that tickled my tongue; bright snappy carrot-stick soldiers.

When I was a teenager my family decamped to New England. Mom's little herb patch was replaced by a rural expanse filled with apple trees. Her new gardens yielded rhubarb in the early spring, and raspberries and blueberries that popped from their buds as the weather grew warmer. In the summer, nasturtiums and zucchini flowers spilled over flagstone walls. Our new way of life dovetailed nicely with Mom's ever-evolving flair for food and cooking. Her gorgeous green salads, lightly tossed with homemade garlic and fresh herb dressing, filled a well-seasoned wooden bowl nightly. Salads came alive for me then.

In college, I spent a year in Paris studying film and photography. I lived on my own in a seventh-floor walkup on the Right Bank. My tiny garret dwelling consisted of a twin bed and small armoire, a tiny wash sink and a single-burner hotplate. I marketed daily, *comme les Parisiennes*, since it was de rigueur and because I didn't have a fridge. Jean-François, my first French friend, shared my passion for cooking and taught me how to make *salade d'endives*. He cut the spear-shaped chicory crosswise into thick crunchy slices and seasoned it simply, with olive oil, a touch of vinegar and good salt. The occasional variation included a sprinkling of toasted walnuts and/or a crumble of creamy Roquefort cheese. Preparing no-fuss elemental salads like this, born out of makeshift necessity and driven by local and seasonal ingredients, quickly became cherished habit.

My fondness for food became my métier. Along with it came other significant salad discoveries: my friend, Sara Jenkins, a talented professional chef, taught me to make fattouche, sharing the brilliant Lebanese technique of mashing garlic with salt then stirring in fresh lemon juice for a rich citrusy dressing without the harsh garlic bite. Watching Italian chef Matteo Boglione prepare his delicious salad of cheese, farro, artichoke and pecorino Toscano in the test kitchen of *La Cucina Italiana* magazine, I learned the joy of a thinly shaved uncooked artichoke. A lifetime of adventurous eating and nearly two decades as a chef, food editor and writer, and yet, I had never eaten a raw artichoke! I love that there is always something new to learn about cooking and eating.

Today, my answer to that impossible question: which one dish would I take to a desert island? A salad. There is no other dish I crave as often, regardless of the season. I continue to be inspired to prepare and eat extraordinary salads every day, a pleasure I'm delighted to share with you.

A couple of navigational notes: Vegetarians, vegans and meat-eaters alike can enjoy this book. Cheese, fish, meat and nuts can generally be eliminated from a recipe and dressings can be swapped to avoid dairy. I hope that this book brings much joy to your salad-making kitchen and that you'll visit me at mindyfox.net to share your salad and other eating adventures or check in on mine.

why a whole book on salad?

In the hectic run-around of my everyday life, I've become adept at throwing together what I call "elemental salads." These few-ingredient salads are often unplanned. I open the fridge and make do with what's there: usually a few offerings that reflect the season. In winter, a lone bulb of fennel, perhaps, with its pretty fronds attached. I thinly shave the bulb, dress it with a healthy drizzle of good olive oil, a grating of lemon zest and a generous squeeze of the juice, then sprinkle it with good salt, coarse pepper and those delicate fronds. Served with a wedge of nice cheese, some grilled bread and a bowlful of olives, my husband Steve and I routinely call this dinner.

Our improvised salads often become favorites, later served to friends and family who delight in their simplicity. "The same can be done with a head of celery!" I hear myself say, instructing to thinly slice the stalks and save those beautiful leaves from the inner heart for sprinkling. "If you happen on an apple, slice that, too. Maybe add a few shavings of Parmigiano-Reggiano and a sprinkle of currants and toasted nuts…" and off I go on my well-worn riff about how to cobble together a super-satisfying weeknight salad from a few arbitrary fridge and pantry bits.

I've always had a natural inclination toward eating healthy foods, but good health is not primarily what inspires me to make salads nor excites me about eating them. Instead it's the seemingly endless possibilities of what the dish can be—everything from a stunningly satisfying and gorgeous plate of raw vegetables dressed with good oil and sea salt to a more complex dish involving ingredients such as fruits, grains, cheese, eggs, fish, meat and more.

Salad is an approachable and appropriate dish at any time of the year. It fits both everyday and lavish occasions, provides punch to a meal of many courses, or serves as a meal on its own. Great salads invite you to dispose of those admonishing health-watch do-and-don't lists and simply enjoy the pleasure of cooking and eating beautiful, healthy, vibrant seasonal food.

thinking beyond greens

Salad often infers a bowl of greens, and a bowl of good greens is indeed delicious. But beyond that bowl, a salad can be so much more. Here's a brief primer on a broader range of salad components.

VEGETABLES AND FRUITS in salads can be all raw, all cooked or a mix of both. Before you start to slice, consider the characteristics of your ingredients. A thinly shaved fennel bulb offers a delicate flavor and texture, while, cut thickly, its anise flavor is more robust. Pickled vegetables and fruits (like carrots or peaches) make great salad ingredients; they can be store-bought or quickly prepared at home (Note: Quick pickles are not preserved, so they should be eaten within a week or so). Dried fruits, like cranberries and raisins, offer pleasing rich- or tart-sweet notes.

GRAINS, LEGUMES AND BEANS bring exceptional nutritional depth to salads, as well as great flavor and texture. These ingredients can play the lead role (a white bean or lentil salad, for example), or be used as an accent in green salads.

NUTS AND SEEDS lend texture, earthy flavor and good fats to a salad. Good fats are monounsaturated and polyunsaturated fats. They're found in high concentrations in nuts, seeds and nut and seed oils.

EGGS, PASTA AND POTATOES are the stalwarts of the salad world. They're also crowd-pleasers and travel well to potlucks, picnics and beach excursions. I've taken a new look at these classics in this book.

FRESH HERBS are among my favorite salad ingredients. I use them liberally, chopped and folded into dressings, sprinkled over the top, or incorporated as whole leaves.

CHEESES OF ALL SORTS—soft, hard, young, aged, mild and/or robust—are delicious and tend to work fantastically in both planned and impromptu salads.

SALT AND SALTY INGREDIENTS like olives, capers and anchovies sometimes announce themselves but often they are used as subtle flavor enhancers.

my seven secrets to extraordinary salads

Like every facet of cooking, making a really good salad involves a little craft and basic know-how. Here are my top seven salad-making tips:

1. SOURCE IMPECCABLY: All good cooking begins with good shopping. This does not necessarily mean breaking the bank: A great salad can be made with just a handful of ingredients, and inexpensive ones at that. What it does mean is choosing your ingredients with care and remaining flexible enough to work with the best of what's available. Purchasing seasonal ingredients at a farmers' market or good-quality food market is ideal—the produce is most often picked the day you buy, and the animal proteins on offer are usually among the healthiest options available. But knowing that you can make a fantastic salad from a few bulbs of quality fennel or a head of sturdy, fresh celery—common year-round, even at most grocery stores—is a great relief when you don't feel like fussing in the kitchen or need to put together an easy, quick dish with ingredients you already have on hand.

Choosing the best of what's available is more important than sticking rigidly to a recipe. Sometimes this means straying from the road map, but with an understanding of basic ingredients it's easy to take good detours. Salad greens, for example, tend to fall into three flavor categories: sweet (including Bibb or Boston, red- and green-leaf lettuces), bitter (radicchio, chicory, frisée, escarole and endive, for example) and peppery (arugula, baby mustard and watercress among them). Most varieties within a flavor category can stand in for one another quite well. Ingredient swaps are not limited to greens. Try a crisp sweet-tart apple in place of a pear, for example, or pitted fresh cherries or a sliced nectarine in lieu of sectioned blood oranges. Each time you stray from or play with a recipe, whether out of necessity or whimsy, your cooking prowess and confidence grows. (For ingredient resources and helpful books on how to choose and prepare fruits and vegetables, see Sources, page 170.)

2. PREP GREENS WITH CARE: Washing, drying, tearing and handling greens gently will help prevent wilting and keep them bright and unblemished for best flavor and good looks. Use a sharp paring knife to trim just the base of head lettuces, then separate leaves. Fill a large bowl (or, for very big batches of greens, a clean sink basin) with very cold water (the temperature is important, as cold water will help perk up greens; add a few ice cubes, if necessary), submerge the leaves, then gently agitate with your hands. Let the greens sit undisturbed for 5 or 10 minutes, during which time dirt and grit will sink to the bottom, then, without agitating so that the grit stays underneath, lift the greens out of the water. If greens are particularly dirty, repeat once or twice with a rinsed bowl or sink and fresh water.

Dry greens in small batches in a salad spinner, then, if you have time, carefully spread them out on a clean dry dishtowel and cover (without pressing) with a second lightweight towel or paper towels to dry more completely. Dressing coats thoroughly dry greens best.

It's generally best to tear large leaves and tender herbs, like basil, by hand, rather than chopping them to prevent bruising, though rinsed and dried basil leaves can also be chiffonaded or thinly sliced.

3. BE SALT (AND PEPPER) SAVVY: A high-quality salt is arguably the single most important ingredient in your kitchen. It pulls forth the flavors of a dish while adding its own characteristic sparkle to both raw and cooked foods. Depending on which type you use, salt also contributes flavor notes of mineral, brine, sweet, sharp, buttery, smoky, floral, fruity and more. Good salts are unprocessed, unrefined and additive-free.

My go-to cooking salt (the one that I use to flavor water for cooking pasta, rice, potatoes and blanched vegetables) is a basic unprocessed fine-grained sea salt. These can be found at most good supermarkets and can often be purchased in bulk. I do spend a bit more of my food budget on unprocessed salt than I would on a common table or kosher salt (both of the latter include chemicals I prefer to avoid), but it is not a budget-breaker. For me, the health and flavor benefits outweigh a bit of added expense.

For seasoning and finishing (a last sprinkle, just before serving), I might use the same basic fine sea salt, or for a more distinctive taste or texture, I keep a

maldon smoked flake salt

fiore di sale di trapani

balinese coarse hollow pyramids

variety of fine-, medium-grained and flaky coarse sea salts on hand. There are no rules as to which one to use when, just a few suggestions.

Fine-grained sea salts are perfect for salad dressings because they incorporate and dissolve well. Medium-grained and flaky sea salts are best for finishing a dish. A few examples of these salts include Maldon or Murray River (crunchy flake salts), and fleur de sel or fiore di sale (Italian fleur de sel). There are dozens of inspiring salts from around the world, and they're becoming more readily available as demand increases. As with wine or olive oil, the best way to become familiar with salts is to taste them.

An important distinction when seasoning is "tasting the salt" in a dish (seasoning appropriately) versus a dish "tasting salty" (oversalting). You do want to taste a salt element in your food; that wonderfully briny, clean pop that makes other ingredients come alive. However, just at the point where you can taste salt and the flavors of the other ingredients in your dish brighten, you have seasoned well and enough. For best success, season gradually, tasting as you go.

A quick word on salt and health: salt is not a "bad" ingredient; we all actually need salt in our bodies to varying degrees. When you cook using high-quality unprocessed ingredients and season with good-tasting unprocessed salt, you're likely to use less salt; your food is being seasoned, not masked, by the salt. Most salt-related health problems do not come from using good-quality salt on unprocessed foods, but rather from eating processed and packaged foods that are loaded with sodium at levels far more than one would use when seasoning unprocessed home-cooked foods. Per dietary requirements, adjust salt in recipes as needed.

When it comes to pepper, black, white and pink peppercorns (which are actually not peppercorns, but

a dried berry) deliver their best flavor when freshly ground or crushed. A good-quality peppermill will allow you to vary your grind from coarse to fine and is a worthwhile investment. The size of your grind (coarse or fine) is a matter of preference, as anything. For a large coarse crush, use the bottom of a small heavy skillet, gently rolling and applying pressure to the skillet over the peppercorns. (For salts and peppers, see Sources, page 170.)

4. LEARN HOW TO SELECT, STORE AND USE OIL AND VINEGAR: I cook primarily with extra-virgin olive oil and generally keep three to four types on hand. The first is a good-quality basic extra-virgin olive oil, which I use for cooking and in some salad dressings. This type of oil is widely available in most supermarkets and has very good basic flavor. To help keep oil-buying economical, I purchase 3-liter cans, transferring the oil (with the help of a $2 mini plastic funnel) to a small, easy-to-grasp glass bottle. I use this basic oil in my more complex salad dressings (those with strong-flavored ingredients, where the nuances of a premium extra-virgin olive oil would be lost) and to cook with.

Heating olive oil does not ruin or rob it of its flavor, but it will diminish the finer characteristics of higher-priced, estate-bottled extra-virgin olive oils. These types of oils are referred to as "finishing oils," because they are most appropriate for drizzling on a dish just before serving. I use these oils in delicately flavored dressings and to drizzle over elemental salads, like those in chapter one of this book.

Finishing oils and specialty vinegars are often marked with the name of an estate, a vintage and/ or a "use by" date, on the label, bottle or bottleneck. Fine olive oils come from Italy, Spain, France, Greece, Morroco, South Africa, New Zealand, California, Chile and beyond. They range in flavor from piquant to mellow (with many nuances in between) and in color from green to gold. The best way to find oils and vinegars that you love is to buy and taste.

Having two or three finer oils, each with different characteristics—one might be peppery, the other grassy or fruity—gives you options to play with. Since it's best to use up premium oils within a year from the time the olives were pressed, and within a few months after opening, I keep only a few oils on hand.

In addition to extra-virgin olive oils, there are nut oils and light neutral-tasting salad oils, like grapeseed. Nut oils and grapeseed oil are very sensitive and can rapidly go rancid after opening. Since I do not use up nut oils quickly, I find it easier to work with nuts than to keep the oils fresh. Heat and light are foes to all oils. When possible, choose oils packaged in tinted glass, and keep bottles stored in a cool, dark place. Store sensitive oils (and nuts, too) in the refrigerator and use them up within a few months after opening.

There are myriad wonderful vinegars to choose from for salad-making. Having a good-quality red and white wine, balsamic and white balsamic, cider and aged sherry vinegar on hand will get you through most of the recipes in this book. When you are buying balsamic vinegars, be sure to purchase those without the words "sugar" and "caramel" in the ingredients. These are low quality and not true balsamics. Wonderful specialty and small-batch vinegars, like Vin Santo vinegar from Italy, are great to add to your basics. When buying specialty vinegars look for those with a stamped lot number and/or best by date (sometimes in fine print or on the back label or neck of the bottle). Store vinegars as you would oils.

5. DRESS FOR SUCCESS: When it comes to dressing salads, my two cardinal rules are avoid bottled dressing and don't overdress. Many of the great salad cultures (Greek, Lebanese, Turkish, Israeli and Italian included) use a simple blend of good olive oil, natural acid (citrus or vinegar) and good salt or salty ingredients, like anchovies or capers. A dressing of this nature can take as little as two minutes to make and is just as convenient, far healthier, more economical and worlds more vibrant-tasting than any commercial dressing you can buy. Most weeknights, I season greens

with fresh lemon juice or a good vinegar and a drizzle of good olive oil. With a little more time, I'll soften and sweeten a tablespoon or two of finely chopped shallot or red onion in vinegar for 10 to 30 minutes, then whisk in oil and season with salt and pepper. A more complex dressing might involve fresh herbs, olives, garlic or crushed or ground dried chiles, like Aleppo pepper or piment d'Espelette. Dressings can go beyond the expected: a pesto can be thinned out with a touch of warm water or extra oil for easy tossing; classic sauces like Italian salsa verde, Turkish tarator and chimichurri make exciting salad dressings as well.

Some cookbooks suggest a 3:1 ratio of oil to acid for salad dressings. I prefer a more flexible approach. The perfect acid-oil balance can change per salad. For example, assertive salad greens, like chicory, might demand a slightly heavier acid hand, whereas a delicate lettuce, like mâche, almost always requires a softer touch. Some salads are best with oil only. Vinegar may vary in acid intensity; personal preference varies as well. While 3:1 is a starting place, being open to variation when making your own dressings often works best. Taste as you go.

To avoid overdressing, use a light coating of dressing on greens, nothing more. If you're unsure of how much to use, add in gradual increments.

6. MIX GENTLY, JUST A BIT AND IN A LARGE WIDE BOWL: Not all salads are tossed, but for those that are, tossing is a critical step in the salad-making process. In just two to three gentle tosses, you want your dressing to lightly coat each ingredient. A large wide bowl is the key to giving your ingredients the space they need to combine in just a few turns, and ensures greens won't bruise.

7. KNOW WHEN TO TOSS: Most rice, bean, potato, pasta and chicken salads improve in flavor when refrigerated for a day or two. But green salads, especially those with delicate or feathery leaves, quickly lose their vitality as they sit. All of your ingredients can be prepped ahead, but toss a green salad only just before serving.

basic tools for extraordinary salads

These tools are my must-haves for salad-making: Fantastic investments, they are useful for other dishes, as well.

BOWLS I use ceramic and wooden bowls for tossing and serving salad. The most important aspect in choosing a salad bowl is its size and shape. Use large, wide bowls (12- to 14-inches, or larger, in diameter); the more people you are serving, the wider and deeper you want your bowl to be. To season a new wooden bowl, rub a small amount of vegetable oil into the grain on the inside of the bowl; repeat every few days for two weeks, then once or twice a year. Avoid using soap to wash wooden bowls, which causes drying and cracking; instead, rinse with very hot or boiling water, then towel and air dry completely before storing.

A set or two of nesting prep bowls, which allow you to measure out and prepare the various ingredients of your recipe is invaluable for salads and other dishes. Prepping an entire ingredient list before tossing or cooking helps you cook better. You'll focus solely on the assembly or cooking rather than dashing back to your cutting board to chop or slice.

A "garbage bowl," one medium bowl for discarding vegetable peels, outer lettuce leaves and other scraps as you prep, makes you a quicker, more focused and neater cook, since you are not constantly walking back and forth from your cutting board to the garbage.

SALTS On my kitchen counter, I keep a sealed jar of unprocessed fine sea salt and another filled with a coarse flaky sea salt; these are the two I reach for daily. Additional specialty finishing salts are stored in sealed containers in my pantry. To serve salts at the table, use small bowls or ceramic dishes, returning salts to airtight containers after each meal to keep them moist and fresh. (See page 10 for more about salt.)

PEPPERMILL Peppermills are like umbrellas—the cheap ones don't tend to work very well or for very long. The flavor of freshly ground pepper is certainly worth the investment of a good mill, and a good one should last a lifetime. I've had great luck with Peugeot mills, which go for $40 to $100 and make a wonderful wedding, birthday or holiday gift. (See Sources, page 170.)

ADJUSTABLE-BLADE SLICER Also called a mandolin or v-slicer, I use my adjustable blade slicer for very thinly slicing vegetables and fruits (hard to do with a knife, especially when you want thin cross-sections of round vegetables, like onions and radishes), and for making matchstick cuts. You can purchase a quality plastic Japanese mandolin for under $40, or you can spend more for a heavy-duty stainless-steel sort. City dwellers will find many types in Chinatown home-goods shops, which are always fun to poke around in. The slicers also have a solid online presence. I've had the same plastic Benriner brand model for years. (See Sources, page 170.)

SHARP KNIVES Every cookbook worth its salt specifies good knives and for good reason. High-quality, well-cared-for knives make a significant impact on the way that you cook. Cutting with precision prevents bruising, which helps keep ingredients fresh. It also ensures your knife won't slip, which helps prevent cuts. There are a lot of great knives out there, each with its own characteristics. Weights and shapes of handles and blades vary, and the best one for you is one that's comfortable in your hand. Test out knives in shops and choose based on comfort. One 6- to 8-inch chef's knife, one paring knife and a good bread knife will cover most home cooks' needs.

SALAD SPINNER This simple, inexpensive tool is widely available, comes in mini and standard sizes and makes quick work of rinsing and drying salad greens and sturdy fresh herbs, like parsley. When I have time, I lay out spun greens on a clean dishtowel for further drying.

CITRUS SQUEEZER This tool is great for getting every last drop of tangy lemon, lime, orange or grapefruit juice out of the fruit and into your salad dressing or juice glass. Sizes and models range from countertop versions (choose from electric and manual) to smaller hand-held devices.

chapter one:

FINISHING YOUR FIRST HOUSE IN MINECRAFT

2 When you first play *Minecraft*, you're probably happy with four walls and a bed, but you quickly start to get more ambitious. Soon enough, you find yourself exploring the world to gather more materials, crafting new tools to collect them, and learning more and more about how *Minecraft* works. By the time you finish your first house, you realize that you've only just begun; there is so much more to do and see. What makes *Minecraft* so great is that you are limited only by your imagination, and it's after you go through that initiation process of finishing your first house that you realize all the possibilities ahead of you.

WORLD 1-1 IN SUPER MARIO BROS.

1 The greatest gaming moment has to be the most iconic level of all time, from the game that helped transform video games into a global phenomenon with its brilliant gameplay and colorful graphics: *Super Mario Bros.* Even people who don't play video games know who Mario is, such was the impact that game had when it hit the NES in 1985. Without world 1-1 of *Super Mario Bros.* to captivate all those imaginations, then, we might not even have half the moments on this list. You can still play the iconic level, since the original game has been released again on Wii U and 3DS.

COMMENT

Jon Gordon
Editor, *gamesTM* magazine

I've loved the *Trials* games since their web-browser days, but the recent *Trials Fusion* was the best yet. I wasn't convinced at first, but the first moment I got some massive air, backflipped with a Superman pose on my bike, and managed to land the front wheel at the last possible moment was breathtaking. After that I was totally hooked. It was just leap, crash, repeat for hours and hours from then on.

And that's even before I got into playing it with friends. Four players leaping, spinning, and bailing across those insane sci-fi tracks was some of the most fun I've had playing a multiplayer game in years. In addition to just surviving the courses and trying to get to the finish line as fast as possible, the final challenge became flinging yourself from your bike before the end. You see, it was faster to leap off your bike at the checkered flag than drive through, but the risk was that if you hit something you would DNF the race completely. Pipping a buddy at the last moment by launching headfirst across the line was the cherry on this insane racing cake of a game.

LEAGUE OF LEGENDS

FULL OF CURIOUS SECRETS . . .

If two champions spend a few seconds dancing in front of Vilemaw on Twisted Treeline, the horrific arachnid will join in by doing the Carlton dance! You can also use the taunt keybind for other cool secrets, such as changing Heimerdinger's walk animation or pulling Rengar's hood down using the Night Hunter skin.

FORZA HORIZON 2

FORZA HORIZON 2

XBOX ONE'S BIGGEST GAME

Microsoft's big exclusive for Xbox One features stunning graphics, tons of championships, and almost 150 music tracks over 7 radio stations. There's plenty to sink your teeth into here, regardless of your driving ability!

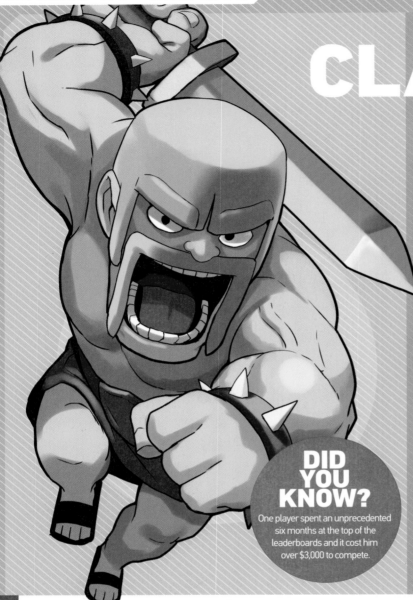

CLASH OF CLANS

TWO TRIBES GO TO WAR

When Supercell formed in Helsinki, Finland, back in 2010, no one expected anything from the small studio. Its first few games—such as *Gunshine* and *Pets vs. Orcs*—certainly didn't suggest great things to come. Then *Clash of Clans* was released in 2012, and it has become a gaming juggernaut, today ranking among the top games in revenue on the App Store and Google Play.

Want to spend your time managing resources and gazing at the gorgeous graphics? Go for it. Do you want to construct a mighty army and unleash a crusade of world domination? You can do that, too. That sort of flexibility has been key to the success of *Clash of Clans*, and we can't wait to see what updates the game will offer next.

DID YOU KNOW?
One player spent an unprecedented six months at the top of the leaderboards and it cost him over $3,000 to compete.

STATS

Generates an estimated
$654,000 in revenue daily

Biggest microtransaction:
£79.99 for 14,000 gems

Star rating from the iOS store (out of 5):
4.5 from 1,945 reviews

Developer Supercell reported
$829 million in revenue in 2014

Estimated 8.5 million daily players

TOP **5** TIPS TO DOMINATE

SAVE YOUR GEMS

1 You might begin *Clash of Clans* with 500 gems, but you will burn through those quickly if you aren't careful enough. Save them early on in the game, as you'll need them later if you want to avoid spending any cash.

TRAIN TROOPS WISELY

2 Look, we know Giants look pretty awesome, but they cost a lot more than a bunch of Barbarians does. Be mindful of the cost (to both resources and time) of your units.

DID YOU KNOW?

Some gamers are so eager to keep playing that they wrap their smart devices in plastic bags so that they can play in the shower!

DEPLOY TROOPS SPARINGLY

3 When you assault a Goblin town, don't drop all your troops in at once. You'll want to spare as many as possible—otherwise, you'll burn through elixir rebuilding your ranks.

TOWN HALL TRICKERY

4 Here's a helpful, little-known trick for you: Don't upgrade your Town Hall too quickly. If your Town Hall is a higher level than your opponent's is, it'll actually reduce the amount of loot you can receive, so it's worth holding back.

START BATTLING EARLY

5 You'll get a three-day shield when you first start playing, but due to your low-level Town Hall, a lot of the big players will just leave you alone. Start matchmaking early and build a reputation.

GET EASY ELIXIR

CHEAT THE SYSTEM

Elixir is the most valuable resource. If you want to get some for free easily, you'll need a barracks (any level), army camp (any level), and laboratory (any level).

CHOOSE AN UPGRADE

Go to your lab and choose a troop to upgrade. Be mindful of the timer. Once the upgrade approaches the 30-second completion timer, go to your barracks, open it, and get ready.

FILL THE BARRACKS

Fill your barracks until your army is full, and then continue building troops. If your camp is full, they'll sit in the barracks until you aren't at capacity. You will need a full army, though.

NOW CANCEL THE UPGRADE!

Once the upgrade is complete in the laboratory, sell back the troops that were in the barracks. You'll receive the upgraded elixir cost, instead of the original amount paid.

CLASH OF CLANS

DID YOU KNOW?

The Clan Wars update that pits players against one another took the team five months to develop. Most updates take only four to six weeks to create!

● When Jorge retired from *Clash of Clans*, he wrote this message to the developers using his base!

● Jorge isn't the only famous player, with Kemal and TETWAH also among the best in the world.

JORGE YAO

WHY? Jorge Yao held the number one spot on the *Clash of Clans* leaderboards for an unprecedented and unmatched six months.

HOW? Jorge Yao became a superfan by playing obsessively. Not only was the world's number one spending over $250 a week on gems, but he was running separate accounts from his North 44 clan to stay ahead.

COMMENT

Alex Trowers
Developer

Be the first or be the best—there was no *Clash of Clans* before *Clash of Clans*. Or, if there was, it had nowhere near the marketing it would have needed to succeed. *Clash of Clans* has a degree of polish that is almost unsurpassed in the mobile space. Just look at the ads, for example—even King, another mobile superpower, had to really up its game to compete. It's also supremely accessible, with a monetization strategy that feels fair and unobtrusive, while the battle layer adds a skill component that goes beyond "tap on thing and wait." All of this is before you get to the social clan war layer, which just adds to the experience.

CLASH OF CLANS

TIME LINE

AUGUST 2012 — *Clash of Clans* launches.

OCTOBER 2012 — It becomes the number one, top-grossing app.

APRIL 2013 — Supercell announces that it's making $2.4 million a day from *Clash of Clans*.

JULY 2013 — Two kids run up $3,000 bill while playing, prompting Supercell to let payments be disabled in-app.

AUGUST 2013 — *Clash of Clans* receives its 14th update and begins releasing monthly weapons and tools.

OCTOBER 2014 — SoftBank and GungHo make a $1.5 billion investment in Supercell to ensure that *Clash of Clans* maintains its popularity.

DECEMBER 2014 — The app breaks into the top 10 on the iOS App Store.

FEBRUARY 2015 — Liam Neeson appears in a *Clash of Clans* commercial during Super Bowl XLIX, further propelling its popularity into the stratosphere.

DID YOU KNOW?

Clash of Clans has become so big that it ran a commercial during Super Bowl XLIX, starring none other than Liam Neeson!

ALSO CHECK OUT . . .

CANDY CRUSH SAGA

The second biggest free-to-play game on iOS. If you're looking for a time suck, you should enjoy this sweet-themed puzzle game that's also hugely popular on Facebook.

VIKINGWARS

VikingWars is a real-time strategy game that gets pretty crazy, pretty quickly. It's a decent clone that's set in Viking times instead of medieval, giving it a fun environment to play in.

CASTLE CLASH

In *Castle Clash*, players have to build great big forts and then send out their powerful heroes to battle other players from around the world. It feels like the logical gameplay extension to *Angry Birds*.

MOBILE ROUNDUP

MOBILE GAMING

DID YOU KNOW?

Titles like *Kingdom Rush*, *Doodle God*, and *Bloons Tower Defense* all started off as browser-based Flash games, and you can still play them now.

THE BEST OF MOBILE!

Mobile gaming is seriously big business. From the moment smartphones gave people the ability to play games on their handsets, developers jumped at the chance to try out new ideas on a new platform—and they've come a long way since *Snake* came preloaded on Nokia phones back in 1998!

It's impossible to talk about mobile gaming without mentioning the gaming colossus that is *Angry Birds*, but there are many more games that are worth downloading to your phone and seeing what they have to offer.

If you're looking for some serious fun, try out *Jetpack Joyride* and play as Halfbrick's hero, Barry Steakfries. If you're more into horror, look no further than *The Nightjar,* in which you'll come up against a terrifying range of monsters that will give you quite a fright. And if you're after something that will test your brain more than your gaming skills, try out the beautifully designed puzzler *Monument Valley.* You won't be disappointed.

STATS

Angry Birds makes
$6 million a month on ads

$11 billion: the predicted amount that will be spent on in-app purchases this year

Over **500 billion** total birds have been shot in *Angry Birds* games

28.2 is the average age of a mobile gamer

67% of all time using tablets is spent playing games

At its peak, *Draw Something* was downloaded **50 million** times in 50 days

TOP **5** FREE GAMES

HEARTHSTONE (2014)

1 Balanced, competitive, and awesome, *Hearthstone: Heroes of Warcraft* is the best free-to-download (with optional in-app purchases) game available on tablets. The greatest part about this card game is that it is extremely easy to pick up and has a nice smooth difficulty curve.

FATES FOREVER (2014)

2 MOBA (multiplayer online battle arena) games are all the rage now, and *Fates Forever* is perhaps one of the most welcoming titles in this genre for newcomers to get sucked into quickly and easily. It's also the best MOBA game currently available on tablets.

TEMPLE RUN 2 (2013)

3 *Temple Run 2* improved on literally everything about its predecessor by adding more characters and hazards, and it is still played like crazy two years after its release. There are countless runner games around, but this has to be one of the best.

ASPHALT 8: AIRBORNE (2013)

4 There is no denying that *Asphalt 8* is the best racing game available on mobile devices. It's tight, it's fast, and it's actually quite ahead of its time, with integrated Twitch streaming so you can broadcast your game session live for other gamers to watch!

SWING COPTERS (2014)

5 Yeah, groan all you like. The successor to *Flappy Bird* is elegant in its simplicity and requires a lot of skill to master, from the timing of the swing to your own anger management abilities! Plus, it's so simple in design that pretty much anyone can give it a try.

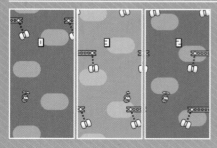

OLD-SCHOOL COOL

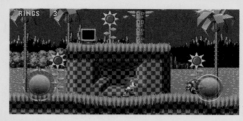

SONIC THE HEDGEHOG
This is a perfect example of *Sonic* at its absolute best, the series original remaining a masterpiece of level design, speed, and creativity. As fun now as it was back then!

METAL SLUG 3
This series was known for its amazing action and gorgeous sprite animation, and now it's available on mobiles. So tie on a bandana, gear up, and go save the world, soldier!

PAC-MAN: C.E.
Pac-Man appeals to pretty much anyone of any age, but let's face it, it can look a little bit dull. *Championship Edition* takes *Pac-Man* and supercharges it with a million volts of electricity.

THE SECRET OF MONKEY ISLAND
Who doesn't love pirates? You should pick this game up just based on the fact that it features a three-headed monkey and a rubber chicken with a pulley in the middle.

MOBILE ROUNDUP

● Steakfries has starred in *Jetpack Joyride*, *Monster Dash*, and *Age of the Zombies*.

BARRY STEAKFRIES

WHO? A mainstay of Halfbrick Studios games, Barry made his debut in *Age of Zombies*, in which he ran around the world, blasting mummies, zombies, and more.

WHY? Given how vast and diverse mobile gaming is, Barry Steakfries is the closest it has to a real mascot. He's starred in his own games, he has his own plot, and he always wears his trademark suit.

COMMENT

Christopher Savory
Creator, *Swap Heroes 2*

I'm extremely proud of *Swap Heroes*. I like how easy it is to grasp the main concept, and I like how quickly the game moves from the player's turn to the enemy's turn and back again. Turn-based strategy games are typically quite slow, so perhaps you could call this an action-turn-based game. I love games that boil it all down and capture a mechanic or experience in as few pieces as possible.

There is a lot of strategy available to the player at any given moment with just four characters. I also think the charming and inviting aesthetic really gets people's attention and brings them into the game.

DID YOU KNOW?
Candy Crush developer King is currently the biggest studio in mobile gaming, earning over $2 billion a year.

ALSO CHECK OUT . . .

KINGDOM RUSH: FRONTIERS

Kingdom Rush started out as a web-browser game. For the smartphone sequel, *Frontiers*, the team paid homage to the original with a free browser version.

CRUSH THE CASTLE

Do you like smashing buildings? Do you like *Angry Birds*? If the answer to either of these question is yes, then check out this classic castle smasher. Using a trebuchet, you get to fling rocks and bombs.

CROSSY ROAD

Just cross the road. Simple, right? Not with all the obstacles that get in your way, such as roads, rivers, and train tracks. There are 89 characters to unlock, from the ordinary (koala) to the bizarre (disco zoo!).

THE BIGGEST MOBILE HITS

1997	SNAKE (NOKIA PHONES)
2000	SNAKE II (NOKIA PHONES)
2003	TOMB RAIDER (N-GAGE)
2004	ASPHALT URBAN GT (N-GAGE)
2007	SONIC THE HEDGEHOG (iOS)
2009	ANGRY BIRDS (iOS/ANDROID)
2010	CUT THE ROPE (iOS/ANDROID)
2011	TEMPLE RUN (iOS/ANDROID)
2011	MINECRAFT POCKET EDITION (XPERIA/iOS/ANDROID/WINDOWS PHONE)
2012	CANDY CRUSH (iOS/ANDROID/WINDOWS PHONE)
2012	CLASH OF CLANS (iOS/ANDROID)
2013	FLAPPY BIRD (iOS/ANDROID)
2014	MONUMENT VALLEY (iOS/ANDROID)

● Anything above 10,000 m in *Jetpack Joyride* is considered an excellent score. But keep going—the highest scores in the world are over 30,000 m!

DID YOU KNOW?

By 2017, mobile gaming will represent 17 percent of all the money that the games industry makes. We've come a long way since the days of *Snake*!

TOP 10 FUNNIEST LINES

DID YOU KNOW?

The NES *Ghostbusters* game caused a stir with its "game completion" screen. It read: "Conglaturation!!! You have completed a great game."

"I AM THE MUSTARD OF YOUR DOOM!"

MARIO & LUIGI: SUPERSTAR SAGA

WHY: The *Mario & Luigi* games, on the whole, are filled with amazing one-liners that will have you constantly chuckling away, the best of which is when boss Fawful screams at you, "I am the mustard of your doom!"

"I AM RUBBER, YOU ARE GLUE"

THE SECRET OF MONKEY ISLAND

WHY: *Monkey Island*'s "I am rubber, you are glue" is one of the many retorts that can be given during its excellent "insult" sword-fighting minigame. You make a fool of yourself in front of the pirate residents.

"A WINNER IS YOU"

PRO WRESTLING

WHY: Coming into existence due to a translation error from the Japanese version of NES game *Pro Wrestling*, the "A winner is you" line appeared on-screen after you beat an opponent. It was adopted by gamers as a term of endearment that's still going strong today.

"THE CAKE IS A LIE"

PORTAL

WHY: No one knows what it means or why it managed to become so popular, but the words "the cake is a lie" scrawled across a wall in *Portal* hit a chord with gamers everywhere. It's seemingly written by one of GLaDOS's former patients who knew more than Chell . . .

"ALL YOUR BASE ARE BELONG TO US"

ZERO WING

WHY: You would think that mistranslated English would be something that only game publishers cared about, but for the second time in our funniest lines list, we're greeted with a language error that is still being quoted by gamers today.

"I TOOK AN ARROW TO THE KNEE"

THE ELDER SCROLLS V: SKYRIM

WHY: On its own merits, "I took an arrow to the knee" isn't really that funny. But when every guard in the game explains that that's the reason he's no longer an adventurer, well, it starts to get a little absurd.

"DO A BARREL ROLL"

STAR FOX 64

WHY: When *Star Fox 64* was released in 1997, few people thought it would be best remembered for a particular line, but just go type the above into Google and see how many results you get. Between animals, helicopters, and soccer players, countless jokes have been inspired due to this one phrase, ensuring that it's as famous, if not more so, than the game itself.

"MARIO!"

LUIGI'S MANSION

WHY: A Nintendo game that focused on Luigi was quite the surprise. Mario's brother usually stayed hidden in the more famous plumber's shadow, so this was his chance to enjoy the spotlight. However, as Luigi crept around a dark mansion in search of his sibling, you could press the A button whenever you wanted to hear the Italian scream out Mario's name in comic fear. It was great!

"UNDER NO CIRCUMSTANCES IS ANYONE ALLOWED TO KIDNAP HER WITHOUT MY SAY-SO!"

PAPER MARIO: THE THOUSAND-YEAR DOOR

WHY: There are usually two goals at the heart of *Mario*: save Princess Peach, defeat Bowser. When a new enemy dared to kidnap the princess, Bowser was less than impressed, taking it so far that he demanded she be returned to her castle . . . so he could kidnap her himself.

"IT'S A-ME . . . MARIO!"

ASSASSIN'S CREED II

WHY: Everyone knows that, for some reason, Mario likes to announce himself at any given moment. What we didn't expect, however, was that Ubisoft's serious *Assassin's Creed* would give a nod to such a famous funny line. The second entry in the series proved us wrong when leader Mario Auditore—who led a group of assassins—introduced himself in such a fashion.

THE EXPERT SAYS . . .
PAUL LYNN
"Smacktalks" on YouTube

The early *Resident Evil* games really paved the way for the survival horror genre, pulling players into dark, scary environments with set camera angles that made it hard to see what was ahead, building on their fear with the groaning sounds in the distance. On top of this, though, it was also unintentionally hilarious due to some of the dialogue not really fitting in with its scary ways. Compliments about picking locks, bizarre remarks about becoming a "human sandwich," nonchalant remarks when someone has just saved your life—*Resident Evil* may be one of the best games ever made, but it's also a little ridiculous.

TOP 10 EPIC RIVALRIES

DID YOU KNOW?

Mortal Kombat was so violent, it led to an official rating system for games. Its biggest rival, *Street Fighter*, had no such effect.

MARIO VS. SONIC

WHY: The best feud in gaming history

No rivalry in games has been as intense or as well publicized as the one between Nintendo's Mario and Sega's Sonic. With both companies trying to outdo each other, nearly every gamer on the planet had to pick a side. The fact that the two now often appear in the same game is unbelievable.

RYU VS. KEN

WHY: Two brothers from another mother

If you didn't know better, you'd be well within your rights to think that *Street Fighter* characters Ryu and Ken were brothers. They dress the same. They have the same moves. They were taught by the same teacher. Amazingly, this isn't the case—and instead, the two are fierce rivals.

SEGA VS. NINTENDO

WHY: Symbol of the early console wars

The war between Mario and Sonic was fueled by the rivalry between the two Japanese companies and their unique consoles. Whereas Nintendo had the NES and Super NES, Sega had the Master System and Mega Drive. All gamers *had* to pick a side. Those were just the rules!

BIRDS VS. PIGS

WHY: Because there can be only one winner . . .

Angry Birds has become one of the biggest games in the world, and a large element of it is the war that has broken out between the birds and the pigs. It all started because the pigs stole some eggs, so the birds decided to try to destroy every pig they could find. A little overboard, but don't expect it to stop soon.

MICROSOFT VS. SONY

WHY: Console wars: round two

As Nintendo went off in its own direction and Sega stopped making consoles, two more companies arrived to wage their own battle: Microsoft and Sony. With the PlayStation finding huge success and becoming the new must-have machine, Microsoft retaliated by releasing the Xbox.

ROCK BAND VS. GUITAR HERO

WHY: The ultimate battle of the bands

At one time, the most popular genre was rhythm action. *Guitar Hero*'s amazing peripheral, which allowed you to hold a guitar, was a breath of fresh air for video games. A new rival soon came to light: *Rock Band*. Throwing in drums and singing, it battled *Guitar Hero* until both ran out of steam.

PES VS. FIFA

WHY: Who really has the best soccer game?

PES was once the best soccer game money could buy. Easily the superior entry to the flashier *FIFA*, Konami's title was the one that "real" soccer fans chose over EA's. And then things changed. Building on its enviable official license, *FIFA* started to improve as a soccer simulator until it was on par with, if not better than, its rival. Today the two are closer than ever, with gamers everywhere arguing each one's merits.

MARIO VS. BOWSER

WHY: Their rivalry has lasted over 30 years

Mario has been trying to defeat Bowser since 1985. That's a ridiculously long time. They've fought all over the Mushroom Kingdom—and even teamed up on occasion—and it's only gotten better as the years have ticked over. Even in *Super Mario 3D World*, the two went at it again and proved there's still plenty more left in the tank. Will Bowser ever win? Unlikely. But that's how we like it . . .

SPYRO VS. CRASH BANDICOOT

WHY: The clashing of two PlayStation mascots

Spyro is now more famous than ever thanks to *Skylanders*, but before that was even a reality, the dragon's game was trying to be number one on Sony's PlayStation. Its rival? Naughty Dog's *Crash Bandicoot*. Even though you could play either game on the console, they continued to clash as they fought for the title of best platformer. It's hard to say who eventually won, but it was an intense time.

FORZA VS. GRAN TURISMO

WHY: The quest for realistic racing

Gran Turismo was the PlayStation's serious racing game. While many racers were happy to be over the top and arcade-y, Polyphony's game made you feel like you were driving a real car. It was an instant success, inspiring numerous rivals, the most triumphant being Turn10's *Forza Motorsport*. Even today this contest continues, with *Gran Turismo 7* and *Forza 6* coming out for the PS4 and Xbox One.

THE EXPERT SAYS . . .
LUKE ALBIGÉS
Editor, *Play* magazine

RYU VS. SAGAT

There are plenty of epic clashes and ancient grudges to be settled in the *Street Fighter* series, but for my money, it's all about the struggle between the iconic poster boy and the towering Muay Thai master. Ken is far too friendly to be a proper rival, but Sagat's vicious approach, imposing figure, and interesting moveset make him perfect for the role. The scar on his chest is timeless proof of his defeat at Ryu's hand at the end of the first game (in which Sagat was the final boss), and there's been a rivalry between the two since both fighters returned in *Street Fighter II*—long may this explosive showdown of fists and fireballs continue!

LITTLEBIGPLANET 3
MAKE YOUR OWN ADVENTURE

Sackboy had already stolen our hearts . . . and then Swoop, OddSock, and Toggle gave us even more faces to fall in love with! Creating your own games with *LittleBigPlanet 3* is surprisingly easy and so much fun.

MINECRAFT

TIME TO BUILD!

Inspired by the likes of *Dwarf Fortress* and *Infiniminer*, Markus "Notch" Persson began working on an idea for a new project known as *Cave Game*. He released the project to the public as an alpha in May 2009 under the new name of *Minecraft* . . . and the rest, as they say, is history! *Minecraft* has grown to become one of the most influential games of all time, from inspiring a flood of copycat titles on Xbox Live to becoming a compulsory subject for some schools in Sweden.

We're now on update 1.8, known as the Bountiful Update, which makes it easier for players to create adventure maps and also added 36 new blocks, included new mobs such as Endermites and Guardians, and rebalanced the repairing and enchanting systems!

DID YOU KNOW?

Minecraft is the most played game on Xbox Live, with over 2 billion hours poured into it so far. That's the same as 230,000 years!

STATS

65 million copies
of the game sold

921.6
quadrillion blocks held in a world

17,900
(on average) playing on the most popular *Minecraft* server

651
different types of blocks and items

256 layers from the top to the bottom

TOP **5** TOUGHEST ENEMIES

CREEPER

1 One of the earlier monsters you will encounter in the game, the Creeper isn't really the toughest to beat. However, his annoying ability to silently sneak up on you and explode—completely ruining your construction—makes this pest a constant pain.

DID YOU KNOW?

Walking to the end of the world in *Minecraft* would take you around 820 hours. Wow— that's a long walk!

ENDERMAN

2 After you've played for a while, these tall, scary creatures will begin to appear. They aren't really threatening at first, but look them in the eyes and they will rush up to you as quickly as they can, even teleporting to get there instantly! It can be very creepy indeed!

GHAST

3 Once you're ready to enter the Nether—bring some extra armor and a sword with you—you'll need to be aware of this creature. In essence, it's a floating jellyfish-like beast that can shoot fireballs. You're better off avoiding this one if you can.

WITHER

4 You won't find a Wither very often, but when you do, you are going to need some of the best armor you can possibly make. A Wither can shoot lots of projectiles at once and can even fly, so you'll probably need a bow if you want to defeat it. Plus, it looks a bit scary, don't you think?

ENDER DRAGON

5 There's only one of these in the game, and you'll have to go on a very long journey to actually encounter it. This flying beast is technically *Minecraft*'s final boss, though in truth you never really finish *Minecraft*.

TOP CREATIONS

1930S NEW YORK

It takes a long time to make any location in *Minecraft*, but the "*Minecraft* Manhattan Project" is especially impressive since its creators built it from images of 1930s-era New York City.

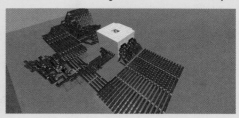

A WORKING COMPUTER

Redstone acts as a sort of circuitry component, usually used to make buttons activate switches. One player used it to make his own functioning computer inside the game!

HOGCRAFT

This mod allows players to use wands and flying brooms, and—with this downloadable map—explore many of the locations seen in the *Harry Potter* films.

ANIMAL CANNON

While it might not be as elaborate as the other projects shown here, it still lets you use dozens of pieces of TNT to fire cows, sheep, or pigs high into the air for comedic effect!

MINECRAFT

DID YOU KNOW?
Telltale Games is working on a narrative-led version of *Minecraft*, similar to its *Walking Dead* and *Game of Thrones* games!

MEET THE SUPERFAN

ARTJOM USMANOV & DMITRY MATVEEV

WHY? These two upload countless custom-made animations about *Minecraft*, from stories involving recognizable characters to music videos about the culture of *Minecraft*.

HOW? These Russian animators—better known by their YouTube channel's name, MineworksAnimations—have been making short videos on *Minecraft* for two years, after gaining almost instant Internet fame with the first of many "Adventures of Steve" animations. They now have millions and millions of views on their videos.

COMMENT

David Trejo
"DavidPlays" on YouTube

Revolutionary games come only once every few generations. I remember explaining to a younger friend how it felt playing *Super Mario 64* for the first time, how great the transition from 2-D to 3-D was. He told me he wished he'd had the chance to witness such a major transition. I told him he had, because he was there for the very early days of *Minecraft*. And not since the transition from 2-D to 3-D has there been such a revolutionary game. I wish more games weren't afraid to steal from it and challenge players to make a game their own.

DID YOU KNOW?
The Danish Geodata Agency re-c[reated]
Denmark in *Minecraft*. Yes, all
square miles (43,000 sq km
It only took 4 trillion bricks
to make it . . .

● Quick tip for you: Right-click on a mooshroom with a bowl and you'll get Mushroom Stew!

● Did you know that the design for the Creeper actually came from a failed model of a pig?

TIME LINE

2011 – MINECRAFT FOR PC
2011 – **MINECRAFT: POCKET EDITION**
2012 – MINECRAFT: XBOX 360 EDITION
2013 – **MINECRAFT: PS3 EDITION**
2014 – MINECRAFT: PS4 & XBOX ONE EDITIONS

ALSO CHECK OUT . . .

LANDMARK
Though there is combat and exploration in *Landmark*, from *EverQuest* creator Daybreak Game Company, the bigger focus is on building with a much more robust and varied set of building tools.

TERRARIA
Here's a game that is very similar in idea to *Minecraft*—explore, mine, upgrade, fight—but with a bigger emphasis on RPG-style combat and boss-style encounters alongside the crafting and building.

STARFORGE
This is slightly more mature than *Minecraft*, but it still offers a similar experience—except that it's a little more science fiction and more spacelike in its overall design.

MARIO

THE KING OF GAMES

If it wasn't for Popeye, we wouldn't have Mario. Back in 1981, legendary video-game creator Shigeru Miyamoto wanted to create a Popeye game, but he couldn't get the Popeye license. Instead, he created Mario as the star of Nintendo's breakout hit *Donkey Kong*, and a legend was born. Since Mario's debut, Nintendo has ensured that each of his releases—whether his own game such as *Super Mario Galaxy* or a spin-off such as *Mario & Sonic at the Olympic Games*—is a game of real quality with the promise of good times to be had.

He's showing no signs of slowing down, either, and has had a busy year, thanks to appearances on Wii U in *Mario vs. Donkey Kong: Tipping Stars*, *Mario Maker*, and *Mario Party 10*. What will the tricky plumber get up to next? We can't wait to find out!

DID YOU KNOW?

Last year's *Mario vs. Donkey Kong: Tipping Stars* is the sixth game in the series that sees the plumber directly take on Donkey Kong!

STATS

Super Mario Bros. has sold

40.24 million copies

20 years: how long Mario has been voiced by Charles Martinet

The main tune from *Super Mario Bros.* has been on the Billboard ringtones chart for

125 weeks

The *Super Mario Bros.* series has produced over

240 million units

Mario has appeared in over

200 games

TOP **5** MARIO GAMES OF ALL TIME

SUPER MARIO WORLD (1990)

1 Some 25 years after release, this is still considered the best *Mario* game of all time and the best platformer ever made. Even if you're playing it today for the first time, it's as much fun now as it was back then!

DID YOU KNOW?

Remember Undodog from *Mario Paint*? The canine pops up in the brand-new *Mario Maker*—only the second time he has appeared in the series to date!

SUPER MARIO 64 (1996)

2 Mario's first fully 3-D outing is still the standard for how to make a 3-D platformer. Exciting, fun, and absolutely brilliant, the game made the plump plumber seem more like a nimble gymnast as he leaped through each level.

SUPER MARIO LAND (1989)

3 Don't fret if you missed out on *Super Mario Land*—one of the best games ever released on Game Boy, with awesome music to go with it—the first time around. You can now buy Nintendo's platformer for your 3DS!

SUPER MARIO GALAXY (2007)

4 Combining *Mario*'s typically brilliant platforming with the Wii's unique controls made for one of the most interesting and exciting *Mario* games ever created—plus it looked absolutely stunning.

PAPER MARIO (2000)

5 Who says Mario is good only in platforming games? Not Nintendo, who managed to squeeze the portly plumber into a superb role-playing adventure as well. This is still one of the best spin-off titles ever made for any gaming series.

COOLEST SECRETS

MARIO KART 8 (Wii U)
You know the speed boost trick when you hit Jump after leaving ramps? You can do this off all environmental hazards! Try the upswelling currents in Dry Dry Desert, for example.

SUPER MARIO 3D WORLD (Wii U)
In World 1-2, grab a green Koopa shell, then hop up onto the platform in front of the brick blocks. Throw the shell, then jump. You will bounce off the shell endlessly, for infinite lives!

SUPER MARIO GALAXY 2 (Wii U)
Think you've mastered this? Not till you've completed the hidden Grandmaster Galaxy! You need to have all 120 green stars and to deposit 9,999 star bits in Banktoad to unlock this level.

SUPER SMASH BROS. (Wii U)
The *Smash* community has agreed on the best characters: Sheik, Diddy Kong, and Rosalina. Donkey Kong, Wii Fit Trainer, and Olimar are considered the worst.

MEET THE SUPERFAN

DID YOU KNOW?

The Boo ghosts in *Super Mario 64* were based on the assistant director's wife, after she exploded with anger at him for spending too much time at work!

MITSUGU KIKAI

WHY? He has the biggest collection of *Mario* items in the world—just take a look above!

HOW? Mitsugu started collecting *Mario* items when he was a baby, starting with a *Mario* cereal bowl bought by his parents. Now he has over 5,400 items and even uses one of the rooms in his two-bedroom apartment in Tokyo solely to house *Mario* memorabilia.

COMMENT

"RetroGamerDaz"
YouTuber

There's a reason why *Mario* is one of the most successful game franchises of all time. Nintendo simply doesn't make bad *Mario* games. Every single *Mario* platformer Nintendo has ever made has pushed the template not only for the franchise, but also for the platform genre in general. *Super Mario 3D World* is currently the best platformer money can buy. Before that it was *Super Mario Galaxy*, before that *Super Mario 64* . . . are you seeing the pattern yet? Mario's name means quality, and even when he turns up in spin-offs, such as *Mario Kart* or *Mario Golf*, they meet his high standards. Mario, we salute you!

TIME LINE

1981 –	DONKEY KONG (ARCADE)
1983 –	MARIO BROS. (NES)
1985 –	SUPER MARIO BROS. (NES)
1988 –	SUPER MARIO BROS. 2 (NES)
1988 –	SUPER MARIO BROS. 3 (NES)
1989 –	SUPER MARIO LAND (GAME BOY)
1990 –	DR. MARIO (NES, GAME BOY)
1990 –	SUPER MARIO WORLD (SNES)
1992 –	SUPER MARIO KART (SNES)
1993 –	SUPER MARIO ALL-STARS (SNES)
1994 –	WARIO LAND (GAME BOY)
1994 –	DONKEY KONG COUNTRY (SNES)
1995 –	MARIO'S TENNIS (VIRTUAL BOY)
1996 –	SUPER MARIO 64 (N64)
1996 –	MARIO KART 64 (N64)
1998 –	MARIO PARTY (N64)
1999 –	SUPER SMASH BROS. (N64)
2000 –	MARIO TENNIS (N64)
2000 –	PAPER MARIO (N64)
2001 –	SUPER SMASH BROS. MELEE (GC)
2002 –	SUPER MARIO SUNSHINE (GC)
2003 –	MARIO KART: DOUBLE DASH!! (GC)
2004 –	PAPER MARIO: THE THOUSAND-YEAR DOOR (GC)
2005 –	MARIO KART ARCADE GP (ARCADE)
2006 –	NEW SUPER MARIO BROS. (DS)
2007 –	SUPER MARIO GALAXY (WII)
2008 –	SUPER SMASH BROS. BRAWL (WII)
2008 –	MARIO KART WII (WII)
2010 –	SUPER MARIO GALAXY 2 (WII)
2011 –	MARIO KART 7 (3DS)
2012 –	NEW SUPER MARIO BROS. U (WII U)
2013 –	SUPER MARIO 3D WORLD (WII U)
2014 –	MARIO KART 8 (WII U)

DID YOU KNOW?

Gaming classic *Super Mario 64* was originally planned for the SNES but got bumped to the Nintendo 64 because the N64 pad had more buttons!

ALSO CHECK OUT . . .

SUPER SMASH BROS.
Mario is part of the all-star cast as Nintendo's biggest characters do battle in one of the funkiest, brightest fighting games ever made. Don't get Mario angry . . . you don't want to see him angry.

RAYMAN LEGENDS
If you miss the 2-D platforming of Mario's past, *Rayman* has come closer to recapturing those glory days than anything else has. Good clean fun that anyone can enjoy.

CAPTAIN TOAD: TREASURE TRACKER
Mario's friend stars in his own outing, a cutesy and effortlessly brilliant adventure that features Captain Toad hunting down treasure.

POKÉMON ™

DID YOU KNOW?

According to Darumaka's Pokédex entry, its droppings are so hot that people used to put them inside their clothes to keep warm!

LET BATTLE COMMENCE!

Gotta catch 'em all!™ *Pokémon*'s motto has stuck around almost since the game started on Game Boy, and all these years later, the series is still going strong! There's the free-to-play *Pokémon Shuffle* that challenges your quick reactions and brainpower; *Camp Pokémon* for your phone teaches you how to become a Pokémon Trainer; and *Twitch Plays Pokémon* was one of the most unusual gaming events of the year, as over 1 million players teamed up to (eventually!) complete *Pokémon Red Version*.

With *Pokémon the Movie: Diancie and the Cocoon of Destruction* impressing the fans, the cartoon series continuing in Kalos, and *Pokémon Rumble World* having just been released for Nintendo 3DS, it'll be a while before this series slows down!

STATS

23.94 million copies of *Pokémon Red Version*, *Pokémon Blue Version*, and *Pokémon Green Version* sold

700 different species of Pokémon

18 Pokémon Types, not including combinations

18 films based on the series

8 Gym Badges needed to face Elite Four

3 first-partner Pokémon to pick from at the start of every game

5 RARE MYTHICAL POKÉMON

MEW

1 This cute creature was so well known for its rarity in the original *Pokémon* games that a wealth of rumors spread about how you could potentially catch it. Despite the speculation, the only legitimate way that you could get your hands on Mew was to get it from special events in Japan.

JIRACHI

2 Much like Mew, Jirachi was attainable only by attending a particular *Pokémon* event where it was being handed out, or from a promotional GameCube disc, and that's still the case to this day. This means that, unfortunately, the only way you'll likely acquire Jirachi is if you trade for it with another Trainer.

DEOXYS

3 Previously, Deoxys could be found only in a very specific way in an earlier *Pokémon* game, but ever since the release of *Pokémon Omega Ruby* and *Pokémon Alpha Sapphire*, you can unlock this rare Pokémon in a secret area after finishing the main portion of the game, making it easier for you to obtain it.

MILOTIC

4 Getting hold of Milotic isn't really the hard part—even if you do need to spend some time leveling your Friendship up. First you are required to go out and catch a Feebas—a fairly pathetic-looking Water-type Pokémon that can be found only in very specific spots throughout the game world.

DARKRAI

5 There was only one place you could find Darkrai, and doing so involved getting your hands on a special in-game ticket directly from Nintendo. After that, the only way you could actually obtain it was through trading with other Pokémon Trainers or by attending special events.

DID YOU KNOW?
Pokémon Drowzee may have been inspired by the tapir, an animal that ate the dreams of sleeping people in Japanese folklore.

COOL LOCATIONS

LUMIOSE CITY
The release of *Pokémon X* and *Pokémon Y* saw the introduction of Lumiose City, the largest city in the Kalos region—and lots of fun to explore!

SECRET BASES
In *Pokémon Ruby Version* and *Pokémon Sapphire Version*, you could build your own base. It's fun to track down the perfect place to call your hideaway and then decorate it!

CELADON GAME CORNER
In the original games, Celadon was a major city and an exciting place to visit—mostly because of its Game Corner, a place where you could play minigames to try to win money!

VICTORY ROAD
This location has appeared in many games. By the time you arrive here, you've defeated every Gym Leader. It's the final challenge before battling the Elite Four.

DID YOU KNOW?

Pikachu's name comes from the noises used in Japan to mean "sparkling" (*pikapika*) and "squeaking" (*chuchu*).

TAMASHII HIROKA

WHY?

Ignoring her YouTube channel full of *Pokémon* videos for a second, Tamashii has also a vast collection of unusual merchandise.

HOW?

Her fandom means that Tamashii has the entire Pokémon Trading Card Game collection, rare games such as the Japanese releases of *Pokémon Red Version* and *Pokémon Green Version* for the original Game Boy, and even items you may not have heard of, such as Pokémon board games. So what's Tamashii's favorite item? None other than a rare Pikachu and Caterpie music box!

COMMENT

Aaron Zheng
Pro gamer

I think that the series has been so successful because the video games are appealing to players of all ages and demographics. My parents were fans of *Pokémon* when I was younger because they thought the game taught good lessons (friendship and teamwork). Pretty much all my friends had one of the *Pokémon* games when we were in elementary school. The games are fun because there are so many aspects to them: collecting and trading Pokémon, building teams, battling, reaching all the achievements in the game . . . There's something in *Pokémon* that appeals to any kind of gamer.

ALSO CHECK OUT . . .

POKÉMON MYSTERY DUNGEON

This series twists the concept of playing as a Trainer capturing Pokémon on its head—instead, you play as popular Pokémon like Pikachu and Charmander.

SUPER SMASH BROS.

This one is a little different, matching up popular Nintendo characters in a four-player free-for-all battle. Different Pokémon have featured as playable fighters here.

POKÉMON SHUFFLE

This *Pokémon* spin-off is free to download on 3DS and features match-three gameplay. Over 3 million *Pokémon* fans have already downloaded and played it, showing how popular it is!

DID YOU KNOW?

Although it doesn't happen in the games themselves, Slowbro is the only Pokémon that can devolve if it loses Shellder on its tail!

TIME LINE

1998 – *POKÉMON RED VERSION* AND *POKÉMON BLUE VERSION*

1998 – *POKÉMON YELLOW VERSION*

2000 – *POKÉMON GOLD VERSION* AND *POKÉMON SILVER VERSION*

2001 – *POKÉMON CRYSTAL VERSION*

2003 – *POKÉMON RUBY VERSION* AND *POKÉMON SAPPHIRE VERSION*

2004 – *POKÉMON FIRERED VERSION* AND *POKÉMON LEAFGREEN VERSION*

2005 – *POKÉMON EMERALD VERSION*

2006 – *POKÉMON DIAMOND VERSION* AND *POKÉMON PEARL VERSION*

2009 – *POKÉMON PLATINUM VERSION*

2010 – *POKÉMON HEARTGOLD VERSION* AND *POKÉMON SOULSILVER VERSION*

2011 – *POKÉMON BLACK VERSION* AND *POKÉMON WHITE VERSION*

2012 – *POKÉMON BLACK VERSION 2* AND *POKÉMON WHITE VERSION 2*

2013 – *POKÉMON X* AND *POKÉMON Y*

2014 – *POKÉMON OMEGA RUBY* AND *POKÉMON ALPHA SAPPHIRE*

TOP 10 GAMING HOAXES

DID YOU KNOW?

GoldenEye is notable for many hoaxes, including a fake cheat that allowed you to play as any James Bond.

PLAY AS LUIGI

SUPER MARIO 64

WHY: Desperate to play as Luigi, gamers decided that a star statue plaque seen in the game's courtyard that read "L is real 2401" meant that if you collected every single coin—of which there were, apparently, 2,401—you'd unlock him. Sadly, it didn't.

FAKE AD

PS4

WHY: Most trailers for new consoles look like they've had millions of dollars piled into them. So when an ad for the PS4 that checked that box was released, gamers thought Sony was ready announce it at that year's E3. As it turned out, the ad was someone's school project!

THE LEGEND OF HEROBRINE

MINECRAFT

WHY: When a creepy screenshot appeared showing a man with bright white eyes, the Internet exploded. Was this a hidden character? An enemy? You could never be sure when he might turn up, but he could appear at any time! Except that he couldn't. Because he wasn't real.

BIGFOOT

GRAND THEFT AUTO: SAN ANDREAS

WHY: Given how big the game was, people started to believe that they might bump into Bigfoot on their travels. But developer Rockstar has denied its existence.

FIGHT WITH SONIC

SUPER SMASH BROS.

WHY: When the game was released, a rumor began, claiming that killing 20-plus enemies in Cruel Melee mode would unlock Sonic as a character. Countless players tried. None succeeded.

SHENG LONG IS HIDDEN IN THE GAME

STREET FIGHTER II

WHY: Started by gaming publication *EGM*, this rumor claimed you could unlock Sheng Long if you played through the game with Ryu, taking no damage and avoiding attacks from M. Bison.

OBTAIN THE TRIFORCE

THE LEGEND OF ZELDA: OCARINA OF TIME

WHY: Why Nintendo decided to preview a shot, showing Link about to get the entire Triforce, before *Ocarina of Time* was released is anyone's guess, but it sent gamers into a frenzy. To their disappointment, no matter how hard you tried, you couldn't get the whole thing.

PS3 REMAKE

FINAL FANTASY VII

WHY: In the buildup to the PS3's release, Sony showed off a tech demo featuring *Final Fantasy VII*'s opening sequence running on its new hardware. This was designed to highlight just how powerful this machine was going to be, but fans everywhere soon decided it meant a full-blown remake was headed to the console. It wasn't . . .

CAPTURING MEW

POKÉMON

WHY: In *Pokémon Red Version* and *Pokémon Blue Version*, the only way to capture Mew was to attend an event where Nintendo gave the legendary Pokémon away. That didn't stop rumors of a way to capture Mew, the most common of which was centered around a truck next to *S.S. Anne* in Vermilion City. But the truck couldn't be moved, and Mew remained elusive.

SAVING AERIS

FINAL FANTASY VII

WHY: Aeris's death in *Final Fantasy VII* is legendary. But what if she could be brought back from the dead? This was the question asked when screenshots appeared of someone fighting the game's final boss with Aeris herself. How was this possible? Well, it wasn't, unless you were happy to hack the game's code and apply Aeris's looks to another character . . .

THE EXPERT SAYS . . .
JAMES STAYTE
Video-game artist

 Mario's gangly brother, Luigi, is always close by in his games, except in *Super Mario 64*. But there were rumors and clues out there . . . A statue in Peach's courtyard has a plaque that reads "L is real 2401." Did it mean I must go to every single level and collect all 2,401 gold coins found in the game? I thought so, and spent hours hunting in every world. Then I ran back to the courtyard, hoping that Luigi would be there waiting, like a present on Christmas morning. I was left disappointed, but the excitement I felt while grabbing all those coins was almost worth it . . .

TOP 10 CUTEST CHARACTERS

DID YOU KNOW?

In *Portal 2*, Chell can creep through a vent and peek at a vast congregation of Turrets who are all singing to their leader—a giant egg-shaped Turret!

PORTAL TURRETS

WHY: *Portal*'s iconic Turrets aren't characters as much as they're objects, but given that they can move (well, kind of) and sing, we're including them anyway. Despite the fact that their main purpose is to destroy you, there's something so sweet and gentle about these merciless killing machines.

SACKBOY

WHY: Even when he's angry, Sackboy is adorable. Though he's a man of few (well, no) words, Sackboy is a master of emotion, able to convey his thoughts with nothing but a well-timed eyebrow arch. Maybe it's the home-crafted look, but there will always be space in our hearts for *LittleBigPlanet*'s leading man.

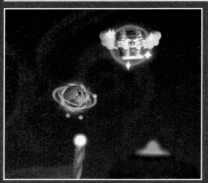

KIRBY

WHY: Bubble-gum pink and twice as sweet, Kirby is unbelievably cute. Is it those round, rosy cheeks? The glowing smile? It's a little of everything, isn't it? Be careful, though—looks can be deceiving. While this pink puffball looks butter-wouldn't-melt sweet, get on his wrong side and you just may get sucked in alive!

ILO AND MILO

WHY: All friends Ilo and Milo want to do is meet by a tree in the park and munch on maple-flavored cookies. However, the lovable two find their daily quest foiled by the complex pathways to each other. It's a very sweet puzzle game, with an even sweeter starring couple!

PIKACHU

WHY: We tried hard not to default to Pikachu when it came to the cutest character contest, but . . . well, just look at it! Not only is it a mascot for all things *Pokémon*, Pikachu is just gorgeous, even in the middle of a battle. It's stuffed with love and fierce loyalty—did you really think we could run a top 10 list like this and not include Pikachu?

YOSHI

WHY: It's difficult to select a favorite from Mario's cast of loyal companions, but there's something special about Yoshi. The plumber's friend has become a key character in an array of *Mario* games, and we think that's due to his mischievous grin, his wide, innocent eyes . . . and his ability to swallow huge dino eggs whole!

ATOI/IOTA

WHY: *Tearaway*'s cast of warm, lovable characters makes it one of the best interactive experiences on the PlayStation Vita. We can't decide if it's the game's rich, colorful backdrop that pleases us, or the innovative, interactive gameplay, but whatever it is, it's impossible not to fall for the charms of the wonderful leading characters—particularly as it's up to us to help them on their journey! It's another cute character set from the makers of *LittleBigPlanet*.

WRECKING BALL

WHY: As with Kirby, there's something about Wrecking Ball's stocky frame and stubby legs that makes him instantly adorable. And as with Kirby, it's probably best not to take this cutie merely at face value. Even though he leaps around like a hyperactive puppy, don't forget that he's one of the most reckless combatants in *Skylanders*—especially when you unleash Wrecking Ball's strongest abilities!

CLANK

WHY: The infamous companion to fellow game namesake Ratchet, Clank is—without exception—the cutest animatronic in the gaming universe. While his oversize green eyes might make him seem a little unwelcoming at first sight, his big grin and unflinching loyalty to Ratchet will soon warm you to him. And to make him even more endearing: He got his name when a ship jolted, causing the tiny robot to hit the side and make a clanking sound.

PIKMIN

WHY: Brought back from the brink of extinction by Captain Olimar (and, apparently, named after his favorite type of carrot, the pikpik), these plant people inhabit the lush world of PNF-404. Standing a proud 1.14 inches (2.9 cm) tall and never hesitant to lend a helping hand when needed, these brightly colored plant-capped wonders show what can be achieved when you band together and work as a team. Now, isn't that just lovely?

THE EXPERT SAYS . . .
MARTIJN BOLK
"Phantaboulous" on YouTube

In my 21 years of gaming, I have seen a lot of cute characters, but I would always go for Kirby! I mean, come on! It's a pink blob! How on Earth can that not be cute?! He wobbles around when he walks, he plays with stars, and he's always so happy! It could be my stomach, but to me he's just like a living ball of cotton candy. And come on, everyone loves cotton candy! Also, his tiny arms are insanely cute, his blushy face is simply adorable, and really he's just a very sweet character overall!

MARIO PARTY

PARTY ON, MARIO!

Hear those screams of frustration as someone's victory is snatched away at the last second? Woken up by the sound of pads clanging against the wall? Then you're in the vicinity of a *Mario Party* player, and the recent release of *Mario Party 10* on Wii U continues the manic multiplayer mayhem in a way few other gaming series dare to match!

Although *Mario Party* is based on a board game, it's actually the minigames that you take part in after each dice roll that contain the true chaos and carnage. Each minigame is designed to be a real test of whether you can be a good winner or good loser—any friendship that can survive the madness within is a friendship you can be truly proud of!

DID YOU KNOW?

Despite its name, *Mario Party 10* will actually be the 13th game in the series, thanks to portable releases such as *Island Tour*!

STATS

There were only

6
playable characters
in the original, compared to . . .

13
playable characters
in *Mario Party 10*

There have been over

8
million sales
of *Mario Party DS*

There are

13
Mario Party
games

TOP **5** MINIGAMES

FRUIT SCOOT SCURRY
(MARIO PARTY 10)

1 A battle to collect fruit doesn't really sound all that exciting, does it? But when players start bumping into one another, there's the potential for some pretty sneaky sabotage!

TUMBLE TEMPLE
(MARIO PARTY 9)

2 If you play the reversed version of this minigame, instead of avoiding the spiked balls, you're racing to hit them. It's weird to have to hurt yourself in order to win, but that's why this is so much fun!

HIDE AND SNEAK
(MARIO PARTY 3)

3 This simple game of hide-and-seek shouldn't be anything special, but it quickly becomes all about the mind games, and about shouting to keep one another from picking the right hiding spots.

PUSHY PENGUINS
(MARIO PARTY 5)

4 Perhaps the most chaotic minigame of them all, this one asks you to try to stay on the ice as penguins try to push you off. How long can you last? That depends on how skilled you are!

BOOKSQUIRM
(MARIO PARTY 4)

5 Book pages slam shut on the players, with the shapes cut into the pages offering the only chance of survival. The shapes get smaller, the pages fall faster ... Who will win? This minigame shines because it's tricky to begin with and gets harder!

TIME LINE

Year	Title
1998	MARIO PARTY
1999	MARIO PARTY 2
2000	MARIO PARTY 3
2002	MARIO PARTY 4
2003	MARIO PARTY 5
2004	MARIO PARTY 6
2005	MARIO PARTY 7
2005	MARIO PARTY ADVANCE
2007	MARIO PARTY 8
2007	MARIO PARTY DS
2012	MARIO PARTY 9
2013	MARIO PARTY: ISLAND TOUR
2015	MARIO PARTY 10

ALSO CHECK OUT . . .

SINGSTAR
Sony's karaoke game is a party favorite, particularly when everyone playing is . . . well, shall we say somewhat musically challenged?

WARIOWARE: SMOOTH MOVES
WarioWare is a series of microgames in which you have to quickly figure out what to do . . . and then do it!

BOMBERMAN
The retro classic is a great game to wheel out at parties—it's simple to play and easy to understand, and the entire game is about devious tactics!

WORLD OF WARCRAFT

THE WOW FACTOR

There aren't many games that have been active for over ten years, but that's what *World of Warcraft* has achieved.

It's not just getting by with the same old gameplay, either, with the recent *Warlords of Draenor* expansion bringing a wealth of new content to explore and play around with—the level cap was raised to 100, players can build and upgrade their own Garrisons, and fans even noticed updates to minute details such as the facial expressions for character models!

There's also the introduction of the *WoW* Token, which allows players to trade gold securely . . . All these changes have added up to keep the world's biggest MMO feeling fresh and new!

DID YOU KNOW?

World of Warcraft is set in Azeroth—among other places—which was also the setting for the three real-time strategy games that came before it.

STATS

Over
500 million
characters created

12 million
subscribers at its peak

Played in
244 countries

619
unique collectible pets

9 million
social guilds created

TOP **5** MOST PLAYED CLASSES

DID YOU KNOW?

Leeroy Jenkins is *WoW*'s most famous player, after a video of him yelling and charging into battle went viral.

DRUID

3 This class is popular because it can play almost every role with ease. Bear form allows Druid to tank. Cat form allows Druid to scout. Entangling Roots and Hibernate allows Druid to crowd control. If you want to fit into any party, pick Druid.

PALADIN

4 This fearsome soldier makes for an awesome tank, as it can build aggro quickly on multiple mobs. Use Righteous Fury to build aggro, followed by either Avenger's Shield or Hand of Reckoning. Use your spell output to keep aggro high during battle.

HUNTER

1 There are two ways of playing a Hunter—either gather up as many vicious pets as you can and use them to decimate your enemies, or focus instead on your ranged weapon to take them down from a distance.

DEATH KNIGHT

2 Although it's unusual, some players prefer to play solo. That's why Death Knight is so popular. The more damage it takes, the more powerful it becomes, making it perfect for a lone warrior.

WARRIOR

5 Focus on building your Strength, Stamina, and Defense stats early on, along with grabbing Plate Armor as soon as possible (try Auction House if none drops), and Warrior becomes an immense member for the front lines of any battle.

COOLEST MOUNTS

SEA TURTLE

This adorable amphibian is actually a very rare mount that you can collect by fishing, which is one of the very many professions you can pick up in the game. You'll certainly need to catch a lot of fish before this guy appears, though.

SPECTRAL TIGER

There are plenty of tiger mounts you can ride in *World of Warcraft*, but if that wasn't cool enough, then why not hop on top of a ghostly equivalent? There are several spectral mounts you can collect, but this has to be the best.

MOTORCYCLE

Though most of the mounts in *World of Warcraft* are animals of some form, there's also a selection of impressive motorbikes you can unlock. You can even get one with a sidecar, so your friend can come along for the ride, too! Looking cool has never been so fun.

ONYXIAN DRAKE

If you manage to defeat one of the toughest bosses in the game, the dragon Onyxia, then there could be a chance that you'll unlock this special mount—a baby Onyxia that you can use to fly around the world in style!

WORLD OF WARCRAFT

DID YOU KNOW?

World of Warcraft took almost five years of development before it released—an extremely long time compared to most games!

ALSO CHECK OUT . . .

WARCRAFT III: REIGN OF CHAOS

For an introduction to how *World of Warcraft* began, you can't go wrong with this, which introduces characters like Arthas and his cursed sword, Frostmourne.

GUILD WARS 2

If—by some miracle—you manage to see everything *World of Warcraft* has to offer, or if you simply feel like a change of scenery, then you'll find a lot to like about *Guild Wars 2*.

HEARTHSTONE: HEROES OF WARCRAFT

Take control of the most important *WoW* characters, but instead of battling it out with swords and shields, this time you'll have a friendly card game.

TIME LINE

Year	Title
1994	WARCRAFT: ORCS & HUMANS
1995	WARCRAFT II: TIDES OF DARKNESS
1996	WARCRAFT II: BEYOND THE DARK PORTAL
2002	WARCRAFT III: REIGN OF CHAOS
2003	WARCRAFT III: THE FROZEN THRONE
2004	WORLD OF WARCRAFT
2007	WORLD OF WARCRAFT: THE BURNING CRUSADE
2008	WORLD OF WARCRAFT: WRATH OF THE LICH KING
2010	WORLD OF WARCRAFT: CATACLYSM
2012	WORLD OF WARCRAFT: MISTS OF PANDARIA
2014	WORLD OF WARCRAFT: WARLORDS OF DRAENOR

COMMENT

Raymond Chris
"HellRa1z3r" on YouTube

World of Warcraft is one of those games I could play while I'm just relaxing, watching TV or something. Unlike a lot of other people, I mainly don't focus so much on the end-game content—I usually spend most of my time questing, or doing something with friends or guild mates. Besides the lore, the social aspect of *World of Warcraft* is one of its biggest strong points, and I believe that's one of the reasons why it's still around today. Until *World of Warcraft* decides to close down on its own, I don't think the game is going anywhere.

MEET THE SUPERFAN

DID YOU KNOW?

WoW developer Blizzard also released a digital card game called *Hearthstone* that allows you to play as heroes from the game.

ANDREW TERRELL

WHY? Andrew's hard work in re-creating an Elven Hunter outfit took hours and hours of research and dedication, but the results paid off!

HOW? Known online as "Jet City Cosplay," Andrew found a second home in Azeroth and the other *WoW* realms, where he made friends from all corners of the world. Now he's met those friends at conventions he's attended in his own *World of Warcraft* cosplay.

DOTA 2

LEAGUE OF ITS OWN

Even though it's tricky to learn, especially compared to *League of Legends*, that hasn't kept *Dota 2* from becoming one of Steam's biggest games—with up to 800,000 players all playing at the same time!

MARIO KART

BLUE SHELL INCOMING!
It's hard to believe, but there was once a time when there were no kart games at all. Then Nintendo decided to pile Mario and his pals onto dinky go-karts, and *Super Mario Kart* was born—and with it an entirely new genre.

Mario Kart 8 kept the traditional mayhem alive—and added to it, with antigravity sections, new items such as the Boomerang Flower, and new characters like Baby Rosalina. Nintendo also pushed out lots of updates to keep *Mario Kart 8* feeling new, such as the brand new 200cc mode, a first for the series. DLC also added new characters from *The Legend of Zelda*, *Animal Crossing*, and more!

DID YOU KNOW?
Kamek the Magikoopa featured in early *Mario Kart 64* screenshots but was dropped. Nearly 70 characters have been featured, but not him!

STATS

There have been
68
playable characters

Mario Kart Wii sold
35.53
million copies
141: number of different tracks in the series

Mario Kart 8's Metacritic score is
88
percent

TOP **5** COURSES EVER

MOUNT WARIO (WII U)

1 Easily *Mario Kart 8*'s best track, this massive single-lap race sees players jumping out of a plane and racing down a huge mountain to see who can reach the bottom first. Awesome fun, as long as you dodge all the shells as you drive through!

BABY PARK (GAMECUBE)

2 Its simple oval shape may make it look like one of the most boring tracks ever, but since it's the smallest *Mario Kart* track, the racers are always close together, and power-ups fly all over the place. This track is absolute carnage.

HYRULE CIRCUIT (WII U)

3 Download the first DLC pack for *Mario Kart 8*, and one of the eight new tracks you'll get is this brilliant tribute to *The Legend of Zelda*. It'll bring back great memories, thanks to the rupees you're collecting and that classic theme music.

BOWSER'S CASTLE (N64)

4 Bowser has had at least one track in every *Mario Kart* game, but this one from *Mario Kart 64* is probably the best because of its castle-roof section and its enormous spiral hallway, perfect for drifting and for really testing your skill.

WARIO STADIUM (N64)

5 Nothing in *Mario Kart* history is crueler than activating a lightning bolt just as someone does the big jump in *Wario Stadium*, causing them to fall and have to do half the track again. Many friendships have broken up over this track . . .

TIME LINE

1992	SUPER MARIO KART
1996	MARIO KART 64
2001	MARIO KART: SUPER CIRCUIT
2003	MARIO KART: DOUBLE DASH!!
2005	MARIO KART DS
2008	MARIO KART WII
2011	MARIO KART 7
2014	MARIO KART 8

ALSO CHECK OUT . . .

SONIC & SEGA ALL-STARS RACING
Sega's answer to *Mario Kart* is a brilliant racer with transforming karts that allow for air, land, and sea travel.

BLUR
Imagine *Mario Kart* with realistic cars and the result is *Blur*, a sadly ignored Xbox 360 and PS3 game that was actually fantastic fun to play.

DIDDY KONG RACING DS
This handheld racer has a great single-player adventure mode, and it will work on your 3DS as well!

MOST COMPETITIVE GAMES

FIFA 15

WHY: *FIFA* has long been a series that has fostered scorching-hot rivalries between friends, but the latest, *FIFA 15*, takes it to a whole new level. How? With emotional intelligence, believe it or not, as players react to everything that happens on the field, from bad tackles to missed shots. It's amazing how this small change amplifies the competition, making the action even more dramatic.

COUNTER-STRIKE: CONDITION ZERO

WHY: Unforgiving for newbies and endlessly playable for those with time to kill, *CS:CZ* is, unsurprisingly, still one of the biggest games on the eSports scene. If you want to see fast-paced action, tune in to any *Condition Zero* tournament on Twitch. Good luck keeping up!

ROCK BAND 3

WHY: *Rock Band* is clever in the way it fosters competitive instincts. You may think you're working together to blast through your favorite music tracks, but you're really trying to prove your musical ferocity. Who's the best musician is a question that can be answered only by the blistering riffs, and with *Rock Band 4* on the way, its competitive legacy will continue.

SUPER SMASH BROS.

WHY: One of the most hard-fought fighting games in the world, *Super Smash Bros.* is intrinsically simple in its design and controls. Capturing the attention of anybody who picks up a game pad and plays, it's random and chaotic in a way that most brawlers aren't, with a huge cast of incredible characters.

ULTRA STREET FIGHTER IV

WHY: Grab *Ultra Street Fighter IV*, the latest in Capcom's long-running series, and experience competition at its hottest! Whether you're screaming in your living room over a perfectly timed hurricane kick or wiping out opponents at a major tournament, there's nothing quite as exhilarating as hearing that final "KO" to signal victory.

LEAGUE OF LEGENDS

WHY: Whether you're playing with friends or pushing to the top of the eSports pile, *League of Legends* is a free-to-play game designed to foster big rivalries once you hit the lanes of Summoner's Rift. It's easy to get involved, but it'll take commitment to get on a level playing field. If you put the time in, however, there are plenty of global tournaments you can join!

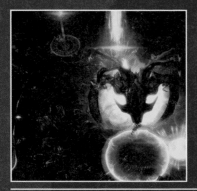

STARCRAFT II: WINGS OF LIBERTY

WHY: For a game that's so complex to wrap your head around at a competitive level, it's surprising to see how huge *StarCraft* remains even today. This is an RTS that brings out the fighting spirit in everyone, where victory can be found only through insane rush techniques and careful multitasking. If you can master *StarCraft*, you can (probably) master anything in life.

MARIO KART 8

WHY: *Mario Kart* has always been one of the games that springs to life when you go head-to-head with others in multiplayer mode. While Nintendo has significantly improved the state of its online services, there's nothing quite like staring somebody dead in the eyes just as that blue shell dashes any hopes they had of a victory—no matter how great the lead they had. It's easy for almost anyone to pick up and play, and fun to master, and that makes *Mario Kart* the reigning king of arcade racers.

DID YOU KNOW?

Despite its simplicity, *Gang Beasts* was crowned one of the best games shown off at recent gaming exhibition Rezzed.

GANG BEASTS

WHY: When this small indie title trickled onto Steam Early Access last year, no one knew what impact it would have on friendships, on relationships, on any and every social interaction. *Gang Beasts* is designed to bring out your devious side, as you try to pick up your friends and throw them to their doom. It's impossible to overstate just how much fun this is and how it will bring out the worst side of you, as you quickly form (and break!) alliances with other players, all to try to gain the upper hand and secure victory.

HEARTHSTONE: HEROES OF WARCRAFT

WHY: *Hearthstone* has made a big impact since its release in March 2014. In fact, not only has Blizzard's free-to-play card battling game surpassed 20 million players worldwide, it has become a huge draw on the eSports scene. It's easy to understand, fun to play, and nearly impossible to master—that's what makes the challenge so enticing. This is one-to-one entertainment like nothing else.

THE EXPERT SAYS . . .
EMMANUEL "CDJR" BRITO
Pro gamer

I think *Super Smash Bros. Melee* is one of the best competitive fighting games out there on the scene, and one of the main reasons for that is the amazing community that has built up around it. It has been around for ten-plus years and is still strong, pulling in big numbers at major tournaments. It just keeps growing and growing, with each tournament and major competitive match truly something to envy.

TOP 10 WEIRDEST GAMES

DID YOU KNOW?

The *WarioWare* series has consistently provided bonkers minigames. Each collection includes a minigame in which you have to pick a massive nose!

HATOFUL BOYFRIEND

WHY: This bizarre romance game puts you in the role of a girl who becomes the first-ever human student at a school for pigeons. As you take classes and get to know your pigeon classmates, they'll slowly start to fall in love with you, and you'll have to choose which one to make your boyfriend. Don't worry, it doesn't make an awful lot of sense to us, either.

GOAT SIMULATOR

WHY: There are all sorts of PC simulator games—farming, truck driving, and the like—but this one takes the cake. In the role of a goat, the player generally gets to walk around and do all manner of goaty things, like lick objects and, um, jump on a trampoline. Weirdly, it seems that a lot of people want to be goats: It's sold over 2.5 million copies to date!

NOBY NOBY BOY

WHY: *Noby Noby Boy* (*noby* means "stretch" in Japanese) is a weird PS3 and iPhone game about a little worm fellow called Boy. By controlling both his front and back sections, you can stretch Boy out really far. The more everyone playing the game stretches, the farther another character called Girl stretches across the universe, unlocking new planets to play on.

TOMODACHI LIFE

WHY: Nintendo's life simulation game lets you add Mii characters to a big block of apartments. Then the madness begins. As the Miis interact with one another, all sorts of crazy stuff happens: One minute you're watching one dream about a ninja, the next you're writing song lyrics for them. It isn't really a "game" as such, more just a collection of weird moments.

BEAT THE BEAT: RHYTHM PARADISE

WHY: The minigames in this collection all have one thing in common: They're played by pressing a button to the rhythm of a beat. Whether you're protecting your date from flying balls or guiding a wrestler through a post-fight interview, it's wacky.

SPEED

40°

BISHI BASHI SPECIAL

WHY: Many arcade games have weird controllers, but *Bishi Bashi Special* kept it simple with three colored buttons. Each of its minigames has you slapping these buttons as you build robots, put together hamburgers, and help a bride throw wedding cake as far as possible at her seated guests.

REVOLUTION X

WHY: There have been countless arcade light-gun games produced over the years, but *Revolution X* from Midway was probably the oddest of them all. In a dystopian version of the '90s, players have to rescue the members of hard rock band Aerosmith, who have been captured by Helga, the leader of an evil, corrupt regime of world police who want to ban music, television, and video games. And to save the bouffant-haired rockers, you need to shoot lots of people with compact discs, apparently. Very bizarre indeed.

SEAMAN

WHY: Sega did some really weird stuff during the days of its Dreamcast console, but *Seaman* was definitely the oddest. It was a virtual-pet game in which you could take care of a giant fish with a man's face, with the game leaving you to figure out how best to look after this odd species. You could talk to Seaman using a special microphone controller, and Seaman would talk back to you. In the English-language version, the giant man-fish was voiced by the late, great Leonard Nimoy, aka Mr. Spock from *Star Trek*.

THE TYPING OF THE DEAD

WHY: Another very odd Sega creation, this was a special version of its light-gun shooter *The House of the Dead* that replaced the gun with a keyboard. As zombies approached, the player had to defeat them by quickly typing out the word or phrase that appeared underneath them. As might be expected, the bosses were much harder to beat; in order to defeat them, the player had to type out full passages instead.

MISTER MOSKEETO

WHY: Thankfully, we don't often find ourselves having to deal with bloodsucking mosquitoes in real life, but that doesn't mean it isn't fun being one in this game. *Mister Moskeeto* has you flying around the house of the Yamadas and sucking blood from them whenever possible. You can't just go in fang first, though: Each individual family member has a stress meter that rises when they spot you approaching, so stealthy sucking is key. It's fun being a little bit of a pest sometimes!

THE EXPERT SAYS . . .
GARETH DUTTON
Games writer & photographer

KATAMARI DAMACY

I reckon the weirdest game is *Katamari Damacy*. The Prince of All Cosmos, who has a head like a giant Christmas cracker, merrily trots about, rolling up everything in the universe into a giant, sticky ball at the request of his dad, the King of All Cosmos. The Prince is tasked with rebuilding the stars after the King accidentally destroyed them all (nice one, Dad). Pencils, pets, people, planets: No object is too big or small to be rolled up into the Prince's jolly ball of terror. A wonderfully weird and hilarious game, *Katamari Damacy* somehow manages to make destroying entire cities, and all life-forms found within, a joyous, light-hearted experience.

DID YOU KNOW?

The very first game—released in 2000—was inspired by a dollhouse, with the "dolls" becoming the virtual characters that you played with.

THE SIMS

VIRTUALLY REAL LIFE

The Sims 4 saw the popular series making a return after a five-year absence, focusing on the emotions of your Sims to make the game feel even more lifelike and adding the brilliant Legacy Challenge, which has you try to keep your Sims family line going through ten generations.

There are also a ton of secrets to discover in *The Sims 4*, such as Sylvan Glade (keep viewing the unique tree in Crick Cabana until your Sim climbs inside) and the bizarre-looking Cowplants (catch a Cowplant berry from the pond near the mine shaft in Desert Bloom Park, then plant it).

The Sims 4 doesn't end there, with expansion packs *Get To Work* and *Outdoor Retreat* adding more fun!

STATS

Over **125** million *Sims* games bought worldwide

11.3 million copies of the original sold in its first two years

The amount every Sim family begins with in *The Sims 4*: **$20,000**

150 objects available to purchase in the original

97 games, spin-offs, and expansion packs released so far

TOP 5 EXPANSION PACKS

DID YOU KNOW?

The Sims was part of a larger series that began with *SimCity*, in which you took control of planning to help a small town grow into a thriving city.

THE SIMS: UNLEASHED

1 *Unleashed* is the biggest-selling expansion pack to date, and rightly so. Not only did it bring the incredibly popular addition of family pets, but you could also visit community locations such as stores and gardening centers.

THE SIMS: VACATION

2 Everyone needs a break from time to time, and Sims are no different. This expansion pack for the original game allowed a family of Sims to travel to one of three different locations: the beach, a forest, or the mountains.

THE SIMS: LIVIN' LARGE

3 This was the first expansion pack for the original game. It didn't add anything in particular, but it did bring a bunch of new items, new characters, and even new careers. Later on, it was also bundled in with the original game.

THE SIMS 2: PETS

4 Because the addition of pets had been so popular in the original game, it was clear that the sequel also needed an expansion pack that allowed pets into the family. This time, they could even get pet-specific jobs!

THE SIMS 2: UNIVERSITY

5 The addition of university was a big deal for *The Sims 2*. It added a whole new generation—young adults—and allowed teenagers to move out and go to college to study one of several different subjects.

GET EASY CASH IN THE SIMS 4

CHEAT CONSOLE

In *The Sims*, the cheat menu is opened by pressing Ctrl, Shift, and C at the same time. If done properly, a small white box will appear at the top of the screen. This is the cheat console.

KACHING

If you type "kaching" into the cheat console when inside a family lot, you'll add an extra 1,000 Simoleons to the bank balance. Entering "rosebud" has the same effect.

REPEAT ENTRIES

To quickly increase your Sims' bank balance, press up on the keyboard while in the cheat console to scroll through previously used cheats, for a big payout without even typing!

MOTHERLODE

If you really want to splash out, you can enter the term "motherlode" into the cheat console while inside a family lot. This will add 50,000 Simoleons to the bank balance!

THE SIMS

DID YOU KNOW?

One of the best-hidden career paths in *The Sims 4* eventually sees you graduate to become an evil supervillain, complete with a Freeze Ray!

COMMENT

Kevin Cornea
"Treesicle" on YouTube

The Sims and its sequels are some of the bestselling PC games of all time, and for good reason. The series has become the clear standard for the simulation genre. The results of the game's innovative lack of an eventual objective are still apparent today. As titles like *Minecraft* grow more popular and influence the next generation of gamers and developers, you must look to *The Sims* as a cornerstone that spurred the creation of such unorthodox and free gameplay.

SASHA AKA VIXELLA

WHY? Sasha's YouTube channel is devoted to *The Sims*, providing daily videos and challenges!

HOW? Vixella, who used to be known as FancySimmer, has quickly risen up the YouTube ranks to become the expert on all things *Sims*. It's all thanks to the staggering number of videos she creates, ranging from simple play-throughs to community-led challenges.

TIME LINE

2000 – THE SIMS
2000 – THE SIMS: LIVIN' LARGE
2001 – THE SIMS: HOUSE PARTY
2001 – THE SIMS: HOT DATE
2002 – THE SIMS: VACATION
2002 – THE SIMS: UNLEASHED
2003 – THE SIMS: SUPERSTAR
2003 – THE SIMS: MAKIN' MAGIC
2004 – THE SIMS 2
2005 – THE SIMS 2: UNIVERSITY
2005 – THE SIMS 2: NIGHTLIFE
2006 – THE SIMS 2: OPEN FOR BUSINESS
2006 – THE SIMS 2: PETS
2007 – THE SIMS 2: SEASONS
2007 – THE SIMS 2: BON VOYAGE
2008 – THE SIMS 2: FREETIME
2008 – THE SIMS 2: APARTMENT LIFE
2009 – THE SIMS 3
2009 – THE SIMS 3: WORLD ADVENTURES
2010 – THE SIMS 3: AMBITIONS
2010 – THE SIMS 3: LATE NIGHT
2011 – THE SIMS 3: GENERATIONS
2011 – THE SIMS 3: PETS
2012 – THE SIMS 3: SHOWTIME
2012 – THE SIMS 3: SUPERNATURAL
2012 – THE SIMS 3: SEASONS
2013 – THE SIMS 3: UNIVERSITY LIFE
2013 – THE SIMS 3: ISLAND PARADISE
2013 – THE SIMS 3: INTO THE FUTURE
2014 – THE SIMS 4
2015 – THE SIMS 4: GET TO WORK

DID YOU KNOW?

Though the language that Sims speak is made up, it was originally based on Ukrainian and a few other languages. It later became known as Simlish.

ALSO CHECK OUT . . .

SPORE
This was sort of the follow-up to *The Sims*, and was much grander in ambition. It let you create an alien life-form and help advance and evolve it through the ages.

ANIMAL CROSSING: NEW LEAF
For a more tranquil approach to life management, see *Animal Crossing*, a game about meeting your neighbors, collecting insects, and decorating a home.

HARVEST MOON: THE LOST VALLEY
A *Harvest Moon* game focuses on elements similar to *The Sims* (building relationships and improving your home) but has more emphasis on farming activities.

HP
5

HP
6

82%
2-3 dmg

MASSIVE CHALICE

USING BRAINS, NOT BRAWN

If you prefer using your gray matter rather than muscle, *Massive Chalice* is a brilliant investment. Only the smartest players survive this turn-based strategy game, which emphasizes resource management over action!

:kback

confirm ?

3

Knockback this target?

end
turn

Caber

Base Damage 5 - 9
Range 1.5

SKYLANDERS

KAOS REIGNS!

As kid-friendly as *Skylanders* appears to be, with its rainbow palette, gorgeous creature design, awesome toy range, and laugh-out-loud script, there's a robust and enjoyable video game here. If you're not immune to the charms of an adventure platformer with plenty of intelligent combat, boss battles, puzzles, secret areas, and collectibles, few games match what *Skylanders* delivers, and fewer still manage to do it so well.

Skylanders: Trap Team, the latest addition to the series, lets you use the brand-new trap item to capture and play as enemies! *Trap Team* also includes Skystones Smash, the strategic sequel to the minigame Skystones . . . but perhaps best of all is the news that a sequel to *Trap Team* is on the way, due for release later this year!

DID YOU KNOW?

The original designs for the game did not include toys coming to life. One of the early ideas was for players to wear special hats.

STATS

Over **175** million *Skylanders* figures have been sold since 2011!

89 was the highest Metacritic score for *Swap Force*

Skylanders is one of the top **20** bestselling game series ever produced

There are around **300** *Skylanders* characters to collect

The rarest *Skylanders* characters are the E3 2011 Trigger Happy, Spyro, and Gill Grunt. They can cost up to **$800** each!

TOP **5** CHARACTERS

BLAST ZONE (FIRE)

1 It would be a mistake to overlook the characters that come with your *Skylanders* starter kit. Able to battle enemies either up close or from a distance, Blast Zone is an excellent all-purpose character that you can use just about anywhere.

DID YOU KNOW?

Before each character is finalized, the *Skylanders* team prints it out in 3-D, to decide what its best pose is.

WASH BUCKLER (WATER)

2 Another character from the starter pack, Wash Buckler offers fantastic offensive and defensive moves and can even trap enemies in bubbles. He also boasts an awesome melee attack!

ZOO LOU (LIFE)

3 We don't love Zoo Lou just because he sports a gigantic club, although that would be reason enough. With excellent combat skills—and the ability to summon a creature to ride and bash into enemies—he's a powerful ally!

BUMBLE BLAST (LIFE)

4 What's better than a strong, powerful Skylander? A strong, powerful Skylander that can shoot bees straight out of his mouth! Yes, you read that right. Employ him in your boss battles for maximum impact!

STAR STRIKE (MAGIC)

5 Not only can the mysterious Star Strike attack multiple enemies and summon allies to shoot beams down from above, he can also deflect and return enemy bullets using his magic shield . . . pretty useful stuff indeed!

SWAP FORCE TIPS

GET THREE STARS ON ALL MAPS

On a Hard/Nightmare mission, choose your bonus mission, and when it starts, switch the difficulty to Easy. You'll have more time to complete and the enemies will be easy!

EIGHT-CHARACTER ENDING

To get every movement/element combo, you need only eight characters. Grab Blast Zone, Wash Buckler, Rattle Shake, Hoot Loop, Free Ranger, and Magna Change from Wave 1— and Rubble Rouser and Stink Bomb from Wave 3.

NIGHTMARE STRUGGLES?

Can't find the Nightmare difficulty mode? Complete the game first, and you'll unlock the Nightmare mode option for your next play-through.

CAN'T FINISH A LEVEL?

Spend time leveling up your Skylanders. Rotate them so that you're using weaker ones in easier parts of the level, then swap for your leveled-up ones when facing boss battles!

SKYLANDERS

DID YOU KNOW?

Do you own Tarclops? Lucky you! Although the character was designed and turned into a toy, it didn't make it into the final game!

ANDY ROBERTSON

WHY? Andy Robertson travels the world to cover *Skylanders* on his Family Gamer TV YouTube channel.

HOW? The creative characters, high-quality sculpts, and sheer variety of limited editions make *Skylanders* the cream of Andy's toy collection (despite the fact that they don't come cheap!).

COMMENT

Laura Dale
Games writer

The *Skylanders* series makes use of colorful, Saturday-morning-cartoon-style mascot characters to present a world that appeals to children who are just getting old enough that they want to get away from "kid stuff," while still being family-friendly enough to be safe for younger players. The series employs a bright, colorful aesthetic and a slapstick sensibility that allow the games to include combat and action, appealing to younger players who want to play games with those elements, while being tame enough in their execution that they're unlikely to cause distress to younger family members.

● Despite being a pirate, Wash Buckler isn't one of the bad guys—he's actually kindhearted!

TIME LINE

2011 – SKYLANDERS: SPYRO'S ADVENTURE
2012 – SKYLANDERS GIANTS
2013 – SKYLANDERS SWAP FORCE
2014 – SKYLANDERS TRAP TEAM

DID YOU KNOW?

To buy every single *Skylanders* character from all four video games would cost you over $3,000! You'd better start saving . . .

● Making sure you have access to all eight elements is one of the keys to success in *Skylanders*.

ALSO CHECK OUT . . .

DISNEY INFINITY

This game has all the fun of portals and figures—plus that special Disney magic! Play as your favorite characters from films, from Sulley and Woody to Mickey and Wreck-It Ralph.

NINTENDO AMIIBO

If you love all things Nintendo, then this is a dream come true. It's a neat little rival to *Disney Infinity*, and you can have plenty of fun and let your imagination run wild.

EPIC MICKEY

Use your Wiimote like a real paintbrush and help Mickey! It's a fantastically fun game for players of all ages.

● Food Fight and Snap Shot are two of the Skylanders you'll start with.

DISNEY INFINITY

THE DREAM TEAM!

If you like the idea of Jack Sparrow teaming up with Buzz Lightyear, Spider-Man, or even Wreck-It Ralph, then *Disney Infinity* is the series for you.

The first *Infinity* borrowed *Skylanders'* idea of collectible toys that can be placed on a portal and sent into your game. Players could collect characters from the likes of *Toy Story*, *Frozen*, and *The Incredibles* and use them in either the Play Sets (stand-alone adventures based on Disney movies) or the *Minecraft*-like Toy Box mode (where anything goes).

When Marvel Comics joined the Disney family, *Disney Infinity: Marvel Super Heroes* added superheroes like the Avengers and the Guardians of the Galaxy to the mix, allowing for even more dream matchups!

DID YOU KNOW?

Lots of characters were planned for *Disney Infinity* but were scrapped. Ferb, Emperor Zurg, and Darkwing Duck all came close to making it.

STATS

So far:

60 figures released

22 Disney and Marvel movies represented

9 different Play Set adventures

Disney Infinity Starter Pack sold over **3** million

TOP **5** PLAY SETS

GUARDIANS OF THE GALAXY

1 Rather than repeating the plot of the movie, this is an all-new Guardians quest that sees you exploring Knowhere and doing missions for Cosmo the dog, Yondu, and the Collector—awesome fun!

THE LONE RANGER

2 You may not have seen the Johnny Depp film it's based on, but this *Disney Infinity* Play Set feels like a Disneyfied version of Rockstar's *Red Dead Redemption*, complete with a train you can hijack! It's the Wild West, but not as you know it . . .

TOY STORY IN SPACE

3 Visit outer space with Buzz, Woody, and Jessie and help out the green aliens while building your own Star Command headquarters. You'll also unlock a jetpack, which can be used to fly around in Toy Box mode.

MONSTERS UNIVERSITY

4 One of the three Play Sets included with the *Disney Infinity Starter Pack*, this has you coming up with all sorts of ways to prank Mike and Sulley's rival school, Fear Tech. Of all the Play Sets to date, this one will make you giggle the most.

THE AVENGERS

5 Featuring the biggest world so far, this Play Set tasks you with stopping Loki from freezing New York. The highlight is soaring through the Big Apple as Iron Man, making you feel every bit as powerful as Tony Stark himself!

PLAY SET TIME LINE

AUG. 2013 –	PIRATES OF THE CARIBBEAN
AUG. 2013 –	MONSTERS UNIVERSITY
AUG. 2013 –	THE INCREDIBLES
AUG. 2013 –	CARS
AUG. 2013 –	THE LONE RANGER
OCT. 2013 –	TOY STORY IN SPACE
SEPT. 2014 –	THE AVENGERS
SEPT. 2014 –	SPIDER-MAN
SEPT. 2014 –	GUARDIANS OF THE GALAXY

ALSO CHECK OUT . . .

DISNEY UNIVERSE
A fun co-op adventure in which players dress up as Disney characters and battle enemies in worlds from *The Lion King*, *Aladdin*, and *Wall-E*.

TOY STORY 3
This was made by the same team that made *Disney Infinity* and has a brilliant Wild West–themed Toy Box mode with hours of missions!

SKYLANDERS TRAP TEAM
If you like collecting figures above all else, Activision's *Skylanders* should be your next port of call!

amiibo

NINTENDO'S TINY ARMY!

The idea of NFC toys that can be used in video games isn't a new one, as anyone who's played *Skylanders* or *Disney Infinity* will agree. But what Nintendo offers with its amiibo figures is something many of its rivals can't: a huge selection of characters that fans already know and love, from Mario and Link to Pikachu and Samus.

Using the built-in NFC reader in the Wii U and the New 3DS, players can use their amiibo to add new content to any game that supports them. This all depends on the game: Scan Donkey Kong into *Super Smash Bros.* to add a CPU-controlled fighter you can level up, or scan Kirby into *Mario Kart 8* to unlock a special Kirby costume for your Mii racer. They're a great way for collectors to add a little something special to their Nintendo games.

DID YOU KNOW?

The NFC technology in amiibo has been around for years. In fact, the Nokia 6131, released all the way back in 2006, was the first phone to use NFC.

STATS

54
amiibo announced to date

A legless Princess Peach sold on eBay for
$25,100

amiibo are
2-4 inches tall

Confirmed to work with
14
games so far

TOP 5 RAREST amiibo

ROSALINA

1 *Super Mario Galaxy*'s Princess Rosalina protects the cosmos and is the adoptive mother of the Lumas—which you can see in the picture! When you collect all 120 stars in *Super Mario Galaxy 2*, a cut scene shows that Rosalina was narrating the entire story to her Lumas.

SHULK

2 The star of *Xenoblade Chronicles*, he differs from most hotheaded JRPG heroes by being calm and collected and thinking things through. Shulk's Monado arts moves such as Speed, Shield, and Buster carried over to his appearance in *Super Smash Bros.*

META KNIGHT

3 With mysterious motives matching his unusual appearance, Meta Knight from *Kirby* has become one of the cult favorites in Nintendo's colorful cast of characters. He's a powerful foe in the new *Super Smash Bros.* outing.

VILLAGER

4 The Villager from *Animal Crossing* was part of the first wave of amiibo released, but he's still pretty hard to find because he's a bit of a cult favorite among Nintendo fans. If you see him in a store, snap him up quickly, because the Villager is very rare indeed!

LITTLE MAC

5 The star of *Punch-Out!!* is rare for one simple reason: Nintendo made him only in limited quantities before the company realized how popular the amiibo craze would be. There may be more coming in the future, but for now, Little Mac's figure is tricky to pin down.

COMPATIBLE GAMES

- SUPER SMASH BROS. FOR WII U & 3DS
- MARIO KART 8
- HYRULE WARRIORS
- CAPTAIN TOAD: TREASURE TRACKER
- MARIO PARTY 10
- ACE COMBAT: ASSAULT HORIZON LEGACY +
- CODE NAME: S.T.E.A.M.
- XENOBLADE CHRONICLES 3D
- STAR FOX FOR WII U
- KIRBY AND THE RAINBOW CURSE
- YOSHI'S WOOLLY WORLD
- SPLATOON

ALSO CHECK OUT . . .

SKYLANDERS: TRAP TEAM
This is the fourth game in the *Skylanders* series, which kicked off the whole "toys in games" craze.

DISNEY INFINITY 2.0
Part action game, part creation game, this combines great Disney characters with Marvel superheroes.

POKÉMON RUMBLE U
This Wii U eShop game lets you scan in tiny *Pokémon* toys, a concept similar to amiibo!

games for beginners

DID YOU KNOW?

It's not just the Wii that offers motion control games—the PS3 and 4, and the Xbox One and 360, offer family-friendly motion-control games, too!

MARIO KART

AVAILABLE ON: 3DS, Wii, Wii U
GENRE: Racing
WHY: Perfect pick-up-and-play controls!

Few games can unite a family as easily as those in Nintendo's infamous racing franchise, *Mario Kart*. With a huge range of characters and racetracks, you'll be spoiled for choice. Simple, easy-to-learn controls and bright, beautiful graphics make *Mario Kart* a hit for beginners and seasoned pros alike, especially since pole position can change faster than you can say, "Banana peel"! Best of all, there's a version available for nearly all Nintendo systems.

MINECRAFT

AVAILABLE ON: Practically everything
GENRE: Adventure
WHY: Let your imagination roam free!

If you can build something with LEGO bricks, you can build anything in *Minecraft*. Let your imagination run riot as you build, explore, and share your worlds, constructing new cities from scratch or re-creating places from your favorite book, show, or film. Yes, there are monsters at night, but disable Survival mode and you'll be able to roam and craft in peace! The only limit to its possibilities is your own imagination. You can carry the whole world in your pocket.

KINECT SPORTS RIVALS

AVAILABLE ON: Xbox One
GENRE: Sports
WHY: Sporty fun for the whole family!

Kinect Sports Rivals gives everyone the chance to join in, even if they've never held an Xbox controller before in their lives. Not all Kinect games are created equal, but *Rivals* is a fun, user-friendly game that allows everyone to take a turn. Boasting everything from bowling and rock climbing to tennis and soccer, there's something for everyone, whether young or just young at heart. Plus, it'll get you on your feet and breaking a sweat!

SKYLANDERS TRAP TEAM

AVAILABLE ON: Practically everything
GENRE: Adventure platformer
WHY: The best introduction to game-pad gaming with portal power!

The *Skylanders* series is not just about cool figurines and portal magic. There's a surprisingly robust adventure platformer beneath the rainbow colors, kooky creatures, and laugh-out-loud story, too. Stuffed with minigames and collectibles, *Skylanders* is the perfect title if you're eager to graduate from motion control to game pad. Experiment with different characters to solve mysteries and battle enemies.

LEGO HARRY POTTER

AVAILABLE ON: Practically everything
GENRE: Adventure
WHY: Fantastic superhero fun!

We've selected *LEGO Harry Potter* because Ron Weasley as a minifigure will always make us giggle, but there are lots of *LEGO* games, including ones for *Star Wars*, *Lord of the Rings*, *Indiana Jones*, and *Batman*. Just select your favorite series and off you go, exploring the jokes, gags, and jam-packed worlds of *LEGO*'s funny, fantastic, and fabulously forgiving in-game universes. The games come with careful tutorials to help you through the controls, and you can co-op it, too, making it the perfect game for matching experienced players with complete beginners.

DISNEY MAGICAL WORLD

AVAILABLE ON: 3DS
GENRE: Adventure
WHY: A safe, magical world to explore!

Disney Magical World is the perfect blend of games like *Zelda* and *Animal Crossing*, with a healthy dose of the always-breathtaking Disney magic. Stuffed with a colorful cast of your Disney favorites old and new—and starring your very own Mii—the game tasks you with collecting a whole range of goodies to help out your friends, including special outfits for each new area. Each world has its own Disney theme, and as your skills and confidence develop, so too does the complexity of your tasks! It's just perfect for all Disney lovers.

POKÉMON ART ACADEMY

AVAILABLE ON: 3DS
GENRE: Tutorial
WHY: It's a creative take on *Pokémon*!

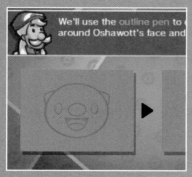

Pokémon Art Academy is not just a great portable game, it's also the perfect opportunity to unleash your inner artist! Encouraging creativity in beginning and experienced gamers alike, it gives you the opportunity to try a whole heap of real-life drawing techniques that will help you draw Pokémon perfectly—and many other things, too! It's not always easy with a stylus and touch screen, we know, but with laugh-out-loud jokes and fantastic tips and tricks, you'll get the hang of it in no time and start creating your very own beautiful masterpieces.

THE HARDEST "EASY" GAME EVER . . . SUPER MEAT BOY

If you want to be challenged by a game that straight-up tests your skill and timing rather than your mastery of finger twisting and complicated controls, then *Super Meat Boy* is ideal. You play a bloody slab of meat trying to make it through the fiendish levels unscathed and in the fastest possible time. With just Run and Jump buttons to help, you need to get past the obstacles—ranging from the predictable, like fire and saws, to the unusual and unexpected, like huge piles of salt! *Super Meat Boy* is notorious for being one of the hardest games ever made, despite having some of the easiest controls to pick up and learn, and anyone who completes it can be considered a true gaming master. Complete this game, and we think you can complete anything.

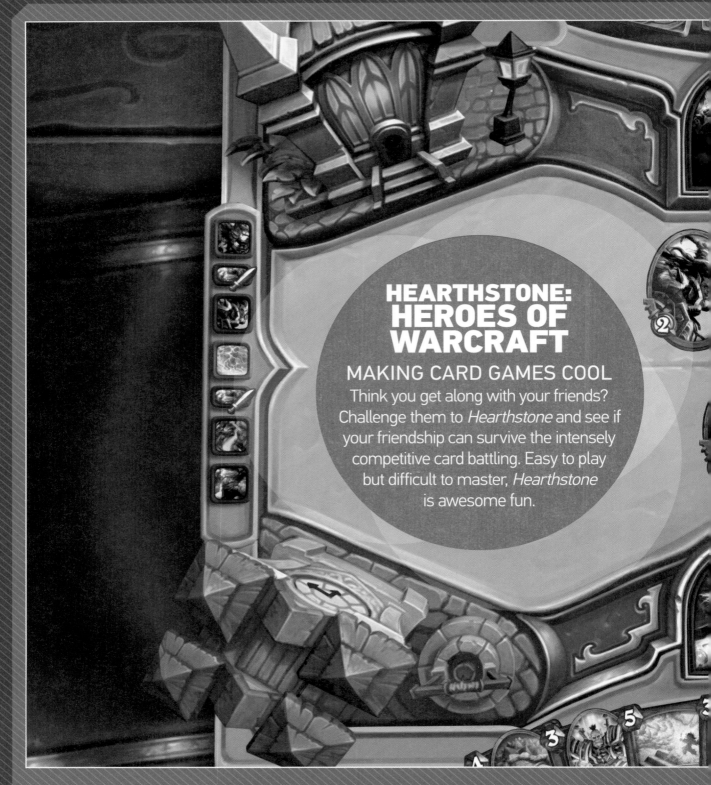

HEARTHSTONE: HEROES OF WARCRAFT

MAKING CARD GAMES COOL

Think you get along with your friends? Challenge them to *Hearthstone* and see if your friendship can survive the intensely competitive card battling. Easy to play but difficult to master, *Hearthstone* is awesome fun.

GLITCHES, STUNTS, AND FAILS

GLITCHES, STUNTS, AND FAILS

MINECRAFT
SPIN ME RIGHT ROUND

It's not often you see the AI in *Minecraft* getting a good workout, but that's exactly what happens here. Occasionally, and for no apparent reason, an animal somehow gets confused and ends up endlessly spinning around on the spot!

DESTINY
BEWARE THE DROP-SHIPS

It happens rarely in *Destiny*, but you can sometimes get taken out by the drop-ships that occasionally swoop past—something we didn't even know was possible until GameFails caught the rare moment on its YouTube channel!

DID YOU KNOW?

Testing games is considered one of the main stepping-stones on the career path toward becoming an actual game designer!

BESIEGE
THE HOME OF TRICK SHOTS

Besiege is a physics-based game in which you have to build medieval siege engines and destroy fortresses. Players are finding ingenious ways to create devastating projectiles, such as this missile . . .

1 The missile has taken off, but how is it going to do anything but travel straight up?

2 A cannon shot followed by an explosion adds the angle needed to hit the target.

3 *KABOOM!* The perfect end for the perfect *Besiege* trick shot!

GLITCHES, STUNTS, AND FAILS

WWE 2K15

THE NOT-SO-GREAT KHALI

The main game featured a ton of amusing bugs, but the DLC brought even more. newLEGACYinc managed to capture some of the best of these, including wrestlers getting stuck in ladders, ridiculous physics fails, and finishers that didn't even work!

LOCOCYLE

THE FIERY MOONWALK

As captured by YouTube channel GameFails, this arcade racer for Xbox One somehow manages to produce an enemy flailing up the road while doing a fiery moonwalk into the distance—a skill we all wish we had on the dance floor!

DID YOU KNOW?

Plants vs. Zombies now has a Taco Bandits game mode, which was added for free last year and involves both sides trying to grab tacos!

PLANTS VS. ZOMBIES GARDEN WARFARE

TAKING THE TRAIN

The brand-new multiplayer maps for *Plants vs. Zombies* include one that has a train running through the middle, a nice bit of decoration to spice up the visuals and keep the game feeling exciting. Except, of course, it's still a train— as this player found out when he blundered right into its path and was quickly taken out as a result!

***Plants vs. Zombies Garden Warfare* has lots of free DLC being released, keeping the cutesy game feeling fresh.**

THE ELDER SCROLLS V: SKYRIM

BOW TIE

This is one of our favorite glitches in games! It doesn't happen too often in *Skyrim*—or rather, most players simply don't notice when it does happen, because they tend to be too busy playing around with the incredibly distracting gameplay. But every now and then, there's a bow ready to fire an arrow . . . even after the archer is long gone!

MADDEN NFL 15

LIKE A PANCAKE

The physics of *Madden* is incredibly realistic, as players' bodies twist and turn when they smash into one another. Sometimes, though, if you catch a player just right, you can flatten him like this!

CITIES: SKYLINES

FLOOD OF TEARS

This *SimCity* rival is already taking players by surprise with its realism. Pinstar uploaded a video showing what happens when you don't take care in building a dam—overflowing causes a flood, leaving a giant mess to clean up.

1 The dam is placed, and you can see the overflow of water to the right. Uh-oh . . .

2 This is the heart-sinking moment when you realize the damage has been done.

3 Anyone got a city-size mop and bucket? Anyone? Please? Help?

GLITCHES, STUNTS, AND FAILS

PEGGLE
THE MILLIONAIRE'S SHOT

1 Want to score several million points with a single *Peggle* shot? First, head to level 11-5.

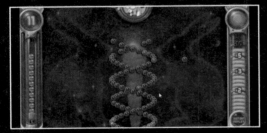

2 Clear a few pegs on the sides, then try to bounce off the wall and then the cup edge.

3 Time it right and the ball will be caught as the pegs at the bottom of the helix close up.

4 All that's left to do is watch as the ball slowly climbs and your score goes crazy!

REIGN OF KINGS
DHALSIM ARMS

Reign of Kings is shaping up to be awesome—you have to hunt wildlife, build weapons, and mine resources to survive in medieval times. Even the glitches are great, such as this villager suddenly developing arms like Dhalsim from *Street Fighter*.

HALO: THE MASTER CHIEF COLLECTION
THE PERFECT SNIPE

Players are falling in love with *Halo 3* all over again, thanks to the recent *Halo: The Master Chief Collection* compilation, and there are new tricks and techniques still being discovered. Lawrencce1 uploaded the perfect snipe on YouTube, one he admits is a lucky shot—a random sniper shot that bounces off three corners before hitting his opponent!

GLITCHES, STUNTS, AND FAILS

THE GOLF CLUB

DEER OH DEER

There's nothing quite like a calm, relaxing game of golf to settle the nerves . . . unless a deer somehow makes its way onto the course! Deer are normally part of the background decoration in *The Golf Club*, but a YouTuber caught a rare moment when a deer appeared on the course. He managed to accidentally hit its leg with his golf ball, which toppled the deer and made his next shot interesting, as you can tell from the screenshot below!

DID YOU KNOW?

After many years and a ton o titles, Rory McIlroy will finally replace Tiger Woods as the cover star of the next EA Sports *PGA Tour* game.

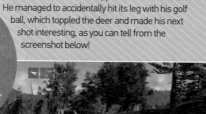

STAR CITIZEN

LEAN WITH ME

Star Citizen is the latest in the current trend of PC games that "grow up" on early access, allowing players to dive in before they see the end product. This means that there are some quirks to be found, such as the leaning glitch that breaks your character's animation when you press E and Q at the same time!

FORZA HORIZON 2 THE DRAMATIC PHOTO FINISH

1 No sign of slowing down as the race is about to end and victory is assured.

2 Uh-oh . . . the smallest clip at high speed means disaster is imminent!

3 A full barrel roll ensues at high speed. Feeling a bit dizzy!

4 The finish line approaches while you're still rolling and crashing . . .

5 . . . and that's as dramatic a finish to a race as you'll ever see!

GLITCHES, STUNTS, AND FAILS

MARVEL VS. CAPCOM 3

COMBOING YOURSELF?

NeoEmpire caught this amazing fail, in which Viewtiful Joe manages to combo himself! His own bomb explodes under him, allowing Deadpool to steal the win. Ouch!

FINAL FANTASY XV: EPISODE DUSCAE

ESCAPING THE DEMO AREA

The *Episode Duscae* demo gives players only a chunk of *Final Fantasy XV*'s world to play in. But if you're hit by a car and knocked over the boundaries, you can go wherever you want! YouTubers have been showing off their findings since launch—here's moreuse's Titan, for instance.

TONY HAWK'S PRO SKATER HD

GRIND FOREVER

The Airport level is infamous among fans, since the baggage claim area allows for near-infinite grinds and huge scores.

DID YOU KNOW?

iRacing currently has over 50,000 members signed up for its subscription service to play online!

IRACING

THE BIGGEST CRASH OF ALL TIME? When physics goes wrong . . .

1 This amazing *iRacing* glitch starts with a huge collision.

2 The unfortunate racer is then sent flying across the track.

3 You'd think this is where the crash ends, but it's only just starting . . .

4 . . . because this crash simply refuses to end, as the car keeps spinning.

5 The car tumbles around by the wall. Then the glitch gets even weirder.

6 Somehow the car starts flipping in the opposite direction!

7 It tumbles back onto the grass where the crash first started.

8 And the car keeps spinning, flipping, and glitching around.

9 Rumor has it the car is still spinning to this day!

FEZ
IT CRASHED?!

One of the coolest things about indie classic *Fez* is the way it plays with expectations. Take the intro, for example. When you first get your fancy new hat, things start to go a little . . . strange. Then everything glitches out and the game "crashes" to a hardware boot screen, before restarting as normal.

SPORTSFRIENDS
3 . . . 2 . . . 1 . . . TAKEOFF!

This brilliant game for PC, PS4, and PS3 is made even better by a glitch that happens in the jousting minigame, in which players get tangled up with each other and their momentum carries them skyward. If only flight was this easy in real life, huh?

FIFA 15
IS IT A FOUL?

The physics engine in *FIFA 15* is so advanced that you can do things with it that (in the spirit of sportsmanship) you're not really supposed to. For example, this moment featuring Paris Saint-Germain striker Zlatan Ibrahimovic . . .

1 The ball is crossed into the box and Ibrahimovic gets ready to control it . . .

2 . . . but a defender gets in the way of his attempt, in the most painful way possible.

3 The game engine does the rest, as the defender is sent flying by the striker's foot!

THE LEGEND OF ZELDA: MAJORA'S MASK

THE CLASSIC LIVES ON

Nintendo rereleased its time-twisting classic *Majora's Mask* on 3DS, and all these years later, whether you're revisiting Termina or playing for the first time, it still stands tall as one of the greatest games ever made.

TOP 10 BOSSES

DID YOU KNOW?

Pigs are the enemy in *Angry Birds* because when the game was being developed, there was a swine flu outbreak across the world!

BOWSER

WHY: There's little doubt that Bowser's success is directly tied to Mario's, but there are few bosses more recognizable or popular than the king of the Koopas. Making his debut in the original *Super Mario Bros.*, Bowser kidnapped Princess Peach and then dared our heroic plumber to come and save her.

M. BISON

WHY: There have been many final foes in the *Street Fighter* series, but no one made as big an impact as M. Bison. With his ambition to control all the world's governments, the dictator has many enemies—from Guile to Ryu to Chun-Li—each of whom entered the Street Fighter tournament to try to best the evil boss.

DR. ROBOTNIK

WHY: Also known as Dr. Eggman, Dr. Robotnik—a mad scientist with an IQ of 300—has been tormenting Sonic for over 20 years. His goal is to construct the Eggman Empire. Obsessed with machinery, Robotnik can always be found in some kind of vehicle as he plots to take over the world.

PSYCHO MANTIS

WHY: *Metal Gear Solid* has always tried to be different, a concept summed up by boss Psycho Mantis. Using his mind-reading abilities, he could instantly counter any strategy a player tried. The solution? Unplug the controller and reinsert it in the second port on the front of the PlayStation!

GANON

WHY: Some of the best boss fights ever have taken place within the *Legend of Zelda* series, and a number of these are due to its main bad guy: Ganon. Whether magically jumping into and out of portraits or turning into a pig monster at the end of *Ocarina of Time*, the leader of the Gerudo makes any battle epic.

WARIO

WHY: Only Nintendo could take Mario's name, change the *M* for a *W*, and make a whole new character based on this premise a success. Yet when he starred in 1992's *Super Mario Land 2: 6 Golden Coins*, Wario was an instant hit. Since then, his evil ways have rarely ceased, but he's found even more popularity thanks to the *WarioWare* series.

CAPTAIN LECHUCK

WHY: The *Monkey Island* games always finish in the same way: a showdown with the ghost pirate LeChuck. A pirate zombie, LeChuck likes nothing more than to construct an army of the undead and then use this crew to try to seize power. He also has a soft spot for Guybrush Threepwood's adventuring partner, Elaine Marley, a woman he constantly tries to kidnap . . . and then marry.

DRACULA

WHY: Dracula has managed to take over most forms of entertainment. Films, books, and television all have famous incarnations of the head vampire, so it was only a matter of time before video games created a version of their own. This happened with Konami's *Castlevania*, an experience that put players in the shoes of monster slayer Simon Belmont and tasked them with doing the unthinkable: killing such a mythical creature.

THE JOKER

WHY: For as long as most people can remember, the Joker has been Batman's archnemesis, a character as famous as the Dark Knight himself. This rivalry extended into the video-game world as well, as the two battled through the *Arkham* series of games to really great effect. The Joker's appearances were so stunning that many people even say that the best version of the character now comes from the video-game space.

DONKEY KONG

WHY: Before Bowser, Donkey Kong was Mario's main rival. Taking a leaf out of Bowser's book and kidnapping a damsel in distress, the ape tried to keep the plumber—then known as Jumpman—at bay by hurling barrels at him in the hope of squashing him flat. Donkey Kong was so popular that Nintendo soon extended his entire family, from Diddy Kong right up to Cranky Kong!

THE EXPERT SAYS . . .
ADAM ELLOHIME
"Ellohime" on Twitch

JON IRENICUS

One sinister antagonist stands above all others in my mind: Jon Irenicus. *Baldur's Gate II* never had me screaming at the top of my lungs in anger, but I remember clearly the eerie way Irenicus slipped between my dreams, whispering tales of my latent powers and making me question the line between genius and madness. He was confident and persistent, and always seemed to be in complete control throughout the story. I felt oppressed and toyed with, the only hope of defeating him lying in unleashing the very powers he sought to manipulate. His presence always seemed to linger, even when I wasn't playing.

FIFA

IN OFF THE POST!

The *FIFA* series is one of the biggest in all of video gaming—it sells millions of copies each year to hungry soccer fans the world over. Developer Electronic Arts has been at the helm of the series ever since *FIFA International Soccer* back in 1993, the first soccer game ever to hold the official FIFA license.

FIFA 15 took the series to a new level, with over 600 emotional reactions from players, ten-man goal celebrations, club-specific chants, and smarter goalkeepers. The increasingly popular Ultimate Team mode also lets users sign loan players for the first time ever. It's difficult to think of what EA could possibly add to the series next—but then again, don't we say that every year?

DID YOU KNOW?

FIFA's Ultimate Team mode has been played by more than 25 million people across all the platforms that it's available to play on.

STATS

The *FIFA* franchise has sold over

100 million copies

57 minutes:

the average amount of time a *FIFA* fan plays the game per day

FIFA games are available in over

51 countries

FIFA is the biggest-selling franchise in EA's history

TOP **5** PLAYERS (according to *FIFA 15*)

LIONEL MESSI
BARCELONA (SPAIN)

1 Leading the charge with an overall rating of 93, Lionel Messi has been ranked the best player of the series for years. He's also constantly considered the best dribbler in the game, with *FIFA 15* giving him a score of 96.

CRISTIANO RONALDO
REAL MADRID (SPAIN)

2 Ronaldo is the runner-up with a score of 92, so any Barcelona vs. Real Madrid encounters mean the two best players in the game are going head-to-head!

DID YOU KNOW?

FIFA allows players to choose which teams they support, and EA says that Real Madrid is the most popular choice.

ARJEN ROBBEN
BAYERN MUNICH (GERMANY)

3 Clocking in with an overall score of 90, Arjen Robben is also tied with Lionel Messi and Cristiano Ronaldo for fastest player in the game, with a whopping score of 93.

ZLATAN IBRAHIMOVIĆ
PARIS SAINT-GERMAIN (FRANCE)

4 Also with a rating of 90, PSG's Zlatan Ibrahimović was ranked the fourth-best player in *FIFA 15*. The Swede also boasts an incredible strength score of 86.

MANUEL NEUER
BAYERN MUNICH (GERMANY)

5 It's not just outfield players who are the best in the game—German goalkeeper Manuel Neuer came in at number five with an overall rating of 90.

FIFA ULTIMATE TEAM TIPS

LEARN THE RULES

A lot of players start Ultimate Team without actually understanding how it all works. Before you even kick a ball, head on over to the FUT website and read up on the basics.

GATHER MORE COINS

Coins are the be-all and end-all in FUT, and the more you have, the more successful you'll be. Trade coins, get boosts, and earn more in order to start as strong as possible.

START TRADING

FUT has a very popular trading community where numerous players are exchanged. Aim to buy relatively cheap players before building them up so you can sell them for a profit.

MAKE CHEMISTRY

It's possible to have a good squad without having the best players, if your player chemistry is high. Keep an eye on your team's chemistry and do your best to improve it.

MEET THE SUPERFAN

FIFA INTERACTIVE WORLD CUP

INTERACTIVE WORLD CUP

9010

VISA
Electron

4000 1294 5678 9010

4000

GOOD THRU
12/16

CHAMPION
USD 20000

VISA
Electron

DID YOU KNOW?

The most popular celebration with *FIFA* players is "Ride the Wave," the trademark dance of Liverpool's Daniel Sturridge.

DAVID BYTHEWAY

WHY? David has won numerous *FIFA* tournaments over the years, and he finished second in the *FIFA* Interactive World Cup in Brazil!

HOW? Starting off just playing in his bedroom for fun, David soon found out that he was highly skilled at *FIFA*, a discovery that was reinforced when other top *FIFA* players told him the same thing. As well as entering multiple tournaments, David also got into eSports and qualified for another FIWC by compiling a record of 100 wins and 0 losses on *FIFA* online.

COMMENT

Chris Bullard
FIFA World Champion

I got into *FIFA* naturally, growing up watching and playing football. As soon as consoles came around, my friends and I would spend all our evenings playing *FIFA* and enjoying it. In the summer of 2004, I was really ill with chicken pox, so I started to play *FIFA* online against friends and other people—come that winter, I was World Champion! I love the competitiveness of it as well as the actual playing. I fancy myself as a good tactician/gamer, so playing *FIFA* is my chance to prove it.

DID YOU KNOW?

64 percent of all players who buy *FIFA* each year will then go on to start a game in Ultimate Team mode.

TIME LINE

1993 – FIFA INTERNATIONAL SOCCER
1994 – FIFA SOCCER 95
1995 – FIFA SOCCER 96
1996 – FIFA 97
1997 – FIFA 64
1997 – FIFA: ROAD TO WORLD CUP 98
1998 – FIFA WORLD CUP 98
1998 – FIFA 99
1999 – FIFA 2000
2000 – FIFA 2001
2000 – FIFA PREMIER LEAGUE STARS
2000 – UEFA EURO 2000
2001 – FIFA FOOTBALL 2002
2001 – FIFA PREMIER LEAGUE STARS 2
2002 – 2002 FIFA WORLD CUP
2002 – FIFA FOOTBALL 2003
2003 – FIFA FOOTBALL 2004
2004 – UEFA EURO 2004
2004 – FIFA FOOTBALL 2005
2005 – FIFA 06
2005 – FIFA STREET
2006 – 2006 FIFA WORLD CUP
2006 – FIFA STREET 2
2006 – FIFA 07
2007 – FIFA 08
2008 – UEFA EURO 2008
2008 – FIFA 09
2008 – FIFA STREET 3
2009 – FIFA 10
2010 – 2010 FIFA WORLD CUP SOUTH AFRICA
2010 – FIFA 11
2011 – FIFA 12
2012 – UEFA EURO 2012
2012 – FIFA 13
2012 – FIFA STREET 4
2013 – FIFA 14
2014 – 2014 FIFA WORLD CUP BRAZIL
2014 – FIFA 15

ALSO CHECK OUT . . .

PRO EVOLUTION SOCCER

The ongoing main competitor to the *FIFA* franchise, Konami's *Pro Evolution Soccer* offers a different experience—but still one that plays a really good game of soccer.

SENSIBLE SOCCER

You'd have to have a retro setup or access to a digital platform to play it, but *Sensible Soccer* remains one of the simplest but most addictive soccer games in history.

FOOTBALL MANAGER 15

For players who'd rather test their managerial skills than see what they can achieve on the actual field, *Football Manager* is, without doubt, the most successful management sim out there.

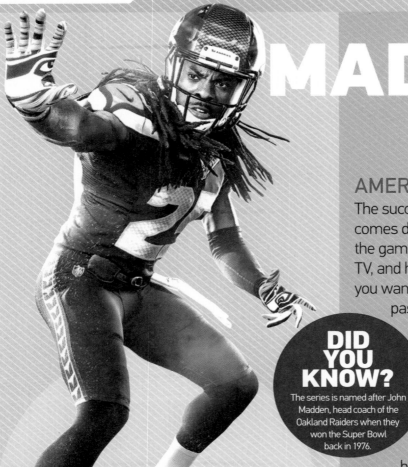

MADDEN NFL

AMERICA'S TOP SPORT

The success of the *Madden* series comes down to how well it re-creates the game-day experience you see on TV, and how it lets you play however you want to. Want to throw monster passes with Aaron Rodgers? Get the ball to Calvin Johnson and let his immense strength and speed do the rest? Maybe just hand the ball to DeMarco Murray and run it at a tired defense? *Madden* allows for all play styles. Even better, *Madden NFL 15* focuses on defensive play, which is often an overlooked part of any sports game. Whether you're throwing the ball or trying to stop it, the end result is that *Madden NFL 15* is ridiculously good fun!

DID YOU KNOW?

The series is named after John Madden, head coach of the Oakland Raiders when they won the Super Bowl back in 1976.

STATS

33 games in the series

Has appeared on **36** different systems

28-24: Super Bowl XLIX's score—correctly predicted by *Madden NFL 15*

Madden NFL was added to the Pro Football Hall of Fame **3** years before the real John Madden was

TOP 5 MADDEN CURSE VICTIMS

DAUNTE CULPEPPER

1 Legend has it that anyone who appears on the cover of a *Madden* game has bad luck. After appearing on *Madden NFL 2002*, Culpepper broke the record for most fumbles in a single season, then injured both his knees.

EDDIE GEORGE

2 Tennessee Titans player Eddie George was the cover star of *Madden NFL 2001*. That season, he lost his team a big play-off game when the ball bobbled out of his hands and was caught by Ray Lewis, who then went on to score.

MICHAEL VICK

3 After being featured on the *Madden NFL 2004* cover, Vick broke his fibula (leg bone) in a preseason match and missed the first 11 games of the season. He was later jailed for setting up illegal dogfights but eventually returned to the NFL.

MARSHALL FAULK

4 The *Madden NFL 2003* star was hit by the curse so badly that not only did he retire early to have knee surgery, but his team—the St. Louis Rams— has been terrible ever since, making the play-offs only twice.

CALVIN JOHNSON

5 Johnson had a great season after appearing on the cover of *Madden NFL 13*, so many people believed the curse had finally been broken. However, he later confessed he'd been playing with three broken fingers the entire season.

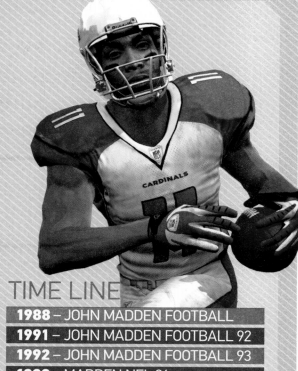

TIME LINE

1988	JOHN MADDEN FOOTBALL
1991	JOHN MADDEN FOOTBALL 92
1992	JOHN MADDEN FOOTBALL 93
1993	MADDEN NFL 94
1994	MADDEN NFL 95
1999	MADDEN NFL 2000
2000	MADDEN NFL 2001
2005	MADDEN NFL 06
2013	MADDEN NFL 25
2014	MADDEN NFL 15

ALSO CHECK OUT . . .

NHL 15
If football isn't your sport of choice, maybe EA's bone-crunching and lightning-quick ice hockey sim will be more to your taste.

NBA 2K15
More of a basketball fan? Go for 2K Sports' fantastic *2K15* instead. Some say it's the best sports game ever.

MLB 14: THE SHOW
If it's baseball you're into, we hope you don't have an Xbox. Sony has the exclusive MLB license, so you can get this only on PS3, PS4, and Vita.

PROJECT CARS

THE MOST REALISTIC RACER AROUND

If you want your racers to be so realistic that you can almost smell the leather interiors, you need *Project CARS* in your life. It has a complex physics system that re-creates the feeling of driving at speed!

WORLD OF TANKS

RUMBLE INTO ACTION

There's no denying it: Tanks are awesome. And the folks at Wargaming know it better than anyone. Since launching in 2010, the company's brilliant free-to-play game *World of Tanks* has built up a player community of millions, thanks to its accessible vehicle combat, wealth of game modes, and staggering range of customization options. The sheer amount of content can be daunting, but the polished visuals, quick-fire action, and balance between vehicles make the game a blast to play. What's more, new tanks, maps, and modes are being added all the time, ensuring that the *World of Tanks* community continues to thrive.

DID YOU KNOW?

World of Tanks set a Guinness World Record in 2012 for number of players online simultaneously on one MOG server, with over 305,000!

WORLD OF TANKS

STATS

The game has won

16

major awards since its debut in 2010

There were over

45 million

registered players in 2012

There are

380

different vehicles currently available in the game

There are over

300

different customizable gun types

80=

Metacritic score

TOP **5** WORLD OF TANKS TIPS

PATIENCE IS A VIRTUE . . .

1 It's worth playing the waiting game, especially if you're in a light tank. Allowing your heavier teammates to inflict a large dose of damage early on will make it much easier for you to nip in for the kill a little bit later.

SPEAK UP, PEOPLE!

2 Talk to your teammates! It might seem obvious, but communication really is key in *World of Tanks*, and knowing exactly what your buddies are up to at all times can mean the difference between victory and defeat.

BE BRAVE, STAND STRONG

3 Don't blink when moving toward an enemy. It might be tempting to turn and flee if you're outnumbered or outgunned, but exposing your sides and rear is a quick way to get yourself blown up.

LEARN TO BLEND IN

4 Camouflage is king in *World of Tanks*. Learn the best hiding spots on each of the maps and try to keep yourself hidden whenever possible. It's obvious, really, but worth remembering: Your enemies can't hit what they can't see.

GET SOME HELP FROM FRIENDS

5 Working alone might be better if you want to stay hidden from opposing artillery, but if you're planning on taking down heavy opponents, it pays to pair up with another member of your team.

TIME LINE

2010 – WORLD OF TANKS

2013 – WORLD OF TANKS BLITZ

2014 – WORLD OF TANKS: XBOX 360 EDITION

2015 – WORLD OF TANKS: XBOX ONE EDITION

ALSO CHECK OUT . . .

WORLD OF WARPLANES
Another of Wargaming's online titles, this one switches the focus from tanks to—you guessed it—planes.

HAWKEN
An intense, free-to-play MMO much like *World of Tanks*, *Hawken* has vehicles that are a variety of armed and mobile walking mechs.

ADVANCE WARS
If you like tanks but want something a little calmer to take part in, Nintendo's *Advance Wars* series offers tank fans turn-based strategy.

NBA 2K15

WHERE AMAZING HAPPENS

It's not just one of the best-looking sports games—*NBA 2K15* is one of the best-looking games ever made. Whether you're going coast-to-coast with John Wall or throwing down nasty Blake Griffin slams, *NBA 2K15* always looks good!

BEST LICENSED GAMES

DID YOU KNOW?

If you leave the character-selection screen inactive in *LEGO Batman 3,* the characters will sing the *Batman* theme!

DUCK-TALES

WHY: Few games encapsulate the spirit of an era as perfectly as *DuckTales.* Taking all that was great about the '80s cartoon and stuffing it with even more awesomeness, courtesy of the people behind the classic *Mega Man* series, this platformer is packed with challenging gameplay.

MARVEL ULTIMATE ALLIANCE

WHY: The characters alone could place *Ultimate Alliance* on this list. Fans of Marvel will have a good time experimenting with the heroic lineup and trying out their special powers. Add in a fun, absorbing story, and what more can you ask for?

LEGO BATMAN

WHY: Maybe it's just because there's something special about seeing this famous cast immortalized as minifigures, but being in the *Batman* universe, LEGO style, is a real treat. There's something particularly bricktastic about *LEGO Batman* that makes it one of the best platformers around.

DISNEY INFINITY

WHY: The only limit to *Disney Infinity* is your own imagination! Choosing from a huge selection of Disney favorites, you can jump in and out of the stories, or tell tales of your own in the game's Toy Box mode. Even when your console's off, you can grab your figures and continue your story off-line!

TOY STORY 3

WHY: *Toy Story 3* came as a surprise. Maybe we just don't expect much from tie-in games, but this one—with its excellent gameplay and sandbox exploration—offers robust gaming, complete with the voices, characters, music, and gorgeous backdrops that you would expect from Pixar's finest.

SCOTT PILGRIM VS. THE WORLD

WHY: Although not based directly upon the film of the same name (released in 2010), this video game offers a distinctive side-scrolling experience that's not just cool to look at but also great fun to play.

EPIC MICKEY 2

WHY: The magic of *Epic Mickey 2* is that you're not just playing the game—you're living it. Using the cutting-edge technology of motion control, you can jump into Mickey's world and once again help him save Wasteland with a wave of your magic paintbrush (and the support of one or two cameo Disney characters, too). It's an absolutely wonderful experience for any Disney fan, whether you're young or just young at heart!

KINGDOM HEARTS

WHY: While we're on the topic of Disney, the *Kingdom Hearts* series offers a mash-up of the very best that the Disney, *Final Fantasy*, and *World Ends With You* franchises have to offer. Set in its own place and time—and available on a whole range of consoles and handheld devices—the series has spawned seven games, and a whole heap of fantastic merchandise, too.

LEGO STAR WARS

WHY: There's a reason we feature so many *LEGO* games! Offering the perfect balance of all things *Star Wars* to satisfy new and hard-core fans alike, *LEGO Star Wars* was the game that kicked off our fascination with the brickification of our favorite franchises. Stuffed with clever characters and laugh-out-loud jokes, this might just be an example of an original and best!

BRAVE

WHY: While *Brave* the video game does touch upon the movie's story line, the narrative takes on a life of its own, following Merida's journey as she chases down her bear-shaped mother (it's a long story). Environments are colorful, engaging, and interactive, and you'll often be rewarded for veering off the beaten path with a sneaky loot chest or three. Simple but effective, *Brave* offers a pretty platform-like experience with simple challenges.

HOW TO BECOME A YOUTUBE STAR

JOSEPH GARRETT
"Stampy" on YouTube

I actually began by trying to become a gaming journalist. When I first started doing videos, I was doing reviews, I was doing guides and top 10 countdowns of things, so that was the route I was trying to get into. I did that for about a year and a half and no one really watched it, but I still did a video almost every single day. During my final year at university and my job, I didn't have time to do that kind of content, so that was the main reason I switched to Let's Play. I was simply able to do a video a day much quicker. That coincided with when *Minecraft* came out on the consoles. I did my first *Minecraft* video in May 2012, and it wasn't immediate, but I noticed that instead of 20 views, I would get 100 views and then 150 views and then a gradual slope leading up from there.

TOP 10 ODDEST ACCESSORIES

DID YOU KNOW?

The Power Glove was featured in the '80s Nintendo movie *The Wizard*, which included these lines: "I love the Power Glove. It's so bad." It certainly is!

DRAGON QUEST SLIME CONTROLLER

WHY: The Slime controller was released alongside Square Enix's *Dragon Quest VIII* on the PlayStation 2. It was both a brilliant sculpture of *Dragon Quest*'s most famous enemy and a fully functioning DualShock 2 controller. Enough to get gamers interested!

DREAMCAST FISHING ROD

WHY: *Sega Bass Fishing* was never going to sell by the bucketload, so Sega created this rather unique motion-sensitive fishing rod controller that was compatible with the game. It also worked with Namco's sword-fighting game *SoulCalibur*. When this news broke, it sold a lot more than expected!

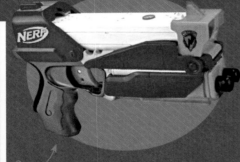

NERF N-STRIKE

WHY: We love Nerf guns because they're a safe way to live out our *Metroid* fantasies. The Nerf N-Strike was a fully functioning foam-dart gun, plus you could also slot in a Wii Remote to create a makeshift Wii Zapper light gun for games like *Link's Crossbow Training*. Brilliant.

CHAINSAW CONTROLLER

WHY: The official *Resident Evil 4* controller, this oddity was too small to look like a real chainsaw but too chainsaw-shaped to be a useful game controller. Still, because they are so unusual, they continue to sell well on eBay to this day.

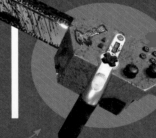

NINTENDO HANDS-FREE CONTROLLER

WHY: Nintendo designed the Hands-Free Controller in the '80s for players who couldn't use their hands. Activity was triggered by a special chin plate and a straw-shaped device that was controlled by mouth actions, in the hope of bringing gaming to everyone.

SAMMY KEYBOARD CONTROLLER GC

WHY: When Sega released *Phantasy Star Online* on the GameCube, players had a dilemma: how to talk to other players. Sammy's Keyboard Controller featured a massive, full-size keyboard. Crazy, but it worked well and did the job it needed to do.

TONY HAWK RIDE SKATEBOARD

WHY: After taking over the world with the fantastic *Guitar Hero* games, Activision decided that big plastic controllers were what people wanted. *DJ Hero*'s turntable controller was brilliant, but this motion-controlled skateboard was a little less popular. The *Tony Hawk* games involved accuracy and perfect trick combos, and the board's sensors and accelerometers proved quite clunky.

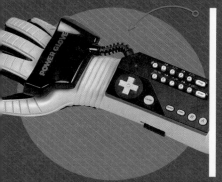

POWER GLOVE

WHY: Long before the Wii Remote existed, toy company Mattel released the Power Glove for the original Nintendo Entertainment System. It was a glove with sensors on the knuckles that could communicate with three other massive sensors that hung off the edge of your TV. The idea was smart but flawed, although a bonus was that you resembled a futuristic robot warrior while wearing the glove!

SEGA ACTIVATOR

WHY: Back when fighting games like *Street Fighter II* and *Mortal Kombat* first arrived on home consoles, Sega came up with a way for gamers to get a little more involved. The Activator was a circular sensor that lay on the ground and sort of halfheartedly converted players' punches and kicks into on-screen attacks. Sega thought gamers would throw out their normal controllers. Unsurprisingly, they didn't.

3RD SPACE GAMING VEST

WHY: For some people, the experience of shooting games just isn't enough, and that's where the 3rd Space Gaming Vest comes in. It might look like a simple piece of attire, but this is a smart vest with an unbelievable secret. Whenever a player wearing the vest is hit in a game, the vest will figure out what direction the hit has come from, and that particular part of the vest will start to vibrate violently!

THE EXPERT SAYS . . .
ROBERT FLORENCE
Glasgow Film Festival gaming ambassador

The weirdest peripheral I own is probably my beloved Para Para Paradise controller for the Japanese PS2 game *Para Para Paradise*. *Para Para* is a Japanese Eurobeat dance craze that is a little bit like line dancing. The accessory is a bunch of plastic pods that you place on the floor; each pod shoots an infrared beam up into the air. As the songs play on-screen, arrows appear in the usual rhythm-game style—but you have to dance using your arms, breaking the infrared beams, in extremely complicated sets of gestures. You look quite mad, but it's wonderful.

THE MOST INFLUENTIAL GAMES EVER

DID YOU KNOW?

The first-ever electronic game was made in 1947 and was influenced by World War II—it looked like radar displays being used at the time!

SUPER MARIO BROS.

WHY: *Super Mario Bros.* is the most influential game of all time. From popularizing consoles to kick-starting the explosion in platformers to crowning Nintendo as the video-game king, *Super Mario Bros.* caused ripples that are still felt today.

METAL GEAR SOLID

WHY: Stealth games had been done before, but none of them was as smart as *MGS*. It was the small touches: guards following footprints, smoke highlighting laser traps, and more. This game showed how cool stealth could be.

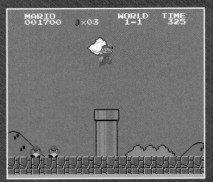

STREET FIGHTER II

WHY: In the early '90s, arcade owners constantly had to fix the sticks on their *Street Fighter II* cabinets, thanks to attempts to pull off spinning pile drivers, spinning bird kicks, and, yes, hadoukens. The game lit competitive fires under all arcade goers.

POKÉMON

WHY: Want to know where the lust for collecting things in *Skylanders*, *Disney Infinity*, and *LEGO Dimensions* came from? You can trace this back to *Pokémon* and its famous "Gotta catch 'em all!" gameplay, in which you tracked down monsters in the wild and captured them for future battles . . . not unlike the hunt for *Skylanders* figures!

PONG

WHY: It's not much to look at—it's little more than two paddles moving up and down, bouncing a ball back and forth. It probably wouldn't hold your attention for more than a few minutes if you were to play it today. But as a moment in history, *Pong* was the first big milestone, announcing the arrival of gaming to the world.

FINAL FANTASY VII

WHY: Although RPGs were already popular, *FFVII* saw the genre explode. It felt like a seismic shift in gaming, thanks to its 3-D visuals, incredible soundtrack, and detailed backgrounds. *FFVII* felt like the first really epic game of the PlayStation era.

GRAND THEFT AUTO III

WHY: Liberty City was more than just the huge playground that *Grand Theft Auto III* took place in. It not only spawned a host of imitators in games like *Saints Row*, *Crackdown*, and the *Arkham* series, it also shifted gaming tastes from linear adventures onto a more open, expansive, and nonlinear level, and really stood out from the crowd.

GRAN TURISMO

WHY: Racing games used to be silly, throwaway affairs that were good fun, but more often than not, no one took them too seriously. *Gran Turismo* changed all that, as it set out to become the most realistic racing game ever. Not only did it inspire other racing games to go down the realism route, but its sweeping success also pushed rival developers to match its obsessive attention to detail.

WIPEOUT

WHY: With Sony as the big newcomer on the block, it needed a big hit to convince gamers that its new PlayStation console was worth buying over its rival, the Sega Saturn. The game that did just that was *WipEout*, an eye-wateringly fast futuristic racer that appealed to nongamers as well as the hard-core gaming crowd, thanks to its sci-fi concept and übercool soundtrack starring the Chemical Brothers and Orbital.

FARMVILLE

WHY: *Farmville* sparked the first social gaming craze, as you built your own farm and sent invites to friends to speed up your progress with growing crops. It might not have been the greatest game ever made, but it didn't matter—the reason it's on this list is that it made the concept of building a "fortress" in social gaming popular. Want proof? You can see how it has since been used in the likes of *Clash of Clans*, *Game of War*, and so on.

THE EXPERT SAYS . . . NICK THORPE
Writer and retro gamer

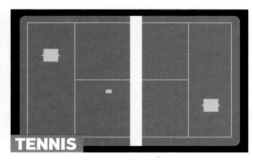

TENNIS

Few of today's gamers have actually played *Tennis* for the aging Magnavox Odyssey, but all of them owe a debt to it. When you play on your Xbox One or your PlayStation 4 or your Wii U today, it's all because of *Tennis*, a game that proved computers could be used for home entertainment and not just as educational machines at universities! And so, because of *Tennis*, the oddly named Magnavox Odyssey became the first-ever games console. Its impact didn't just stop there, either. Nolan Bushnell was an entrepreneur who had already tried to enter the games industry and flopped with *Computer Space*. When he saw *Tennis* running for the first time, he decided to try again, this time by founding a company that released a very similar game into the arcades. That company was Atari and that game was *Pong*. The rest, as they say, is history.

LEAGUE OF LEGENDS

WORLD'S BIGGEST MULTIPLAYER GAME?

League of Legends has continued its unstoppable rise—it remains the most popular game on Twitch, and Jinx and Yasuo have been added to the huge roster of champions.

LEAGUE OF LEGENDS

LET BATTLE COMMENCE

By taking the competitive nature of fighting games and matching it with a top-down view and a *huge* roster of characters, *League of Legends* has managed to become the biggest game in the world, streaking ahead of the likes of *Counter-Strike* and *Hearthstone* on Twitch and even hosting gaming tournaments where pro gamers can earn millions in winnings! It really is all about that selection of characters, with each having its own unique attributes and abilities that affect how your whole team plays. It's tricky to learn, but *League of Legends* is that rare game that is free to play, has tons of depth, and doesn't have demanding PC requirements. Get sucked in!

DID YOU KNOW?

During peak hours, over 7.5 million gamers play *League of Legends* at the same time. It's certainly easy to find online matches!

STATS

Every month,

67 million players

Latest tournament entrants played for

$2.13 million

30,000 monthly viewers, on average, for Bjergsen's Twitch *League of Legends* stream

Playable champions:

123 and rising

TOP 5 LOL CHAMPIONS

THRESH

1 This reaper of souls is the most popular *League of Legends* champion thanks to his huge hook, a weapon that he is able to toss into a group of enemies, either to hold one of them in place or to pull himself into the middle of battle. While Thresh's Damnation ability gains power over time, he does start off relatively weak.

GRAVES

2 This bearded fellow is capable of dealing out a lot of damage thanks to his variety of powerful ranged attacks, making him one of the biggest offensive threats in any team. The fact that he can quickly dash across short distances and create a smoke screen to avoid enemies makes him even more dangerous!

LEONA

3 There aren't many characters who can take down Leona. This heroic champion benefits from excellent health and armor stats, and she is perfectly suited to brawling with multiple enemies at once. She often throws herself into an ongoing brawl, stunning anyone who even thinks of trying to escape.

DID YOU KNOW?
GE Tigers of Korea, Edward Gaming of China, Team SoloMid of North America, and SK Gaming of Europe are the best *League* teams in the world!

LEE SIN

4 Otherwise known as the blind monk, Lee Sin is capable of some truly incredible acrobatic moves. With excellent speed and a devastating attack stat, he has the ability to be a huge threat in almost any team. Just because he can't see, that doesn't mean he can't hit you.

CAITLYN

5 Caitlyn's cheeky British attitude nicely complements her sharpshooting skills, as she uses her sniper rifle to bring down enemies from a distance. If you're low on health, Caitlyn will be there to finish you off, but catch her at close quarters and her low health means it won't take much to take her down.

BEAT YOUR RIVALS

GET GOLD
The easiest way to make sure you win is to collect the most gold, which is best done early on by "last hitting." This means making sure you get the final attack on an enemy minion.

BUY ITEMS
With that gold, you can return to base and spend it on items for your character. There are plenty to choose from, though the recommended options are usually the best.

KILL THE DRAGON
On the bottom side of the river, you'll find a dragon. Once you and your team are higher levels, you can attempt to kill this beast in order to gain a huge benefit to your team.

DESTROY TOWERS
The key here is to obliterate your enemy's base, but you'll need to wipe out their towers first. Teaming up will help you destroy towers quickly, but remember to defend your own!

LEAGUE OF LEGENDS

DID YOU KNOW?

League of Legends was inspired by Defense of the Ancients, a custom map made for *Warcraft III: The Frozen Throne* in 2005.

GIULIETTA ZAWADZKI

WHY? Giulietta's love of the *League of Legends* character Akali is apparent from her handcrafted Blood Moon Akali costume.

HOW? As a child, Giulietta loved dressing up. Now she studies art, using her creative skills to make fantastic costumes based on her favorite video-game characters, as well as attending conventions.

COMMENT

Kadeem Mundy
Cosplayer

League of Legends is no longer just a game to me, it's more like a culture now. Before, *League* was just a quick pastime I'd play after class with friends, but now a lot of my life happens to intertwine with it. Aside from playing it, I cosplay from it; the *League* cosplay community is pretty big, and we're always following the new updates from the game to somehow incorporate it in our art. I'm also a pretty big fan of the official *League of Legends* Championship Series, the teams, and how they're sort of converting the game into a sport. It's always fun watching my favorite teams play and rooting for them, just like someone would with other sports.

● Katarina is agile and mobile, making her one of the sneakier and trickier champions to use.

● Mordekaiser is great for those who like to fight at close range.

● With his high health, Volibear is great in one-on-one battles, making him a good choice for top lane or jungle.

ALSO CHECK OUT . . .

DOTA 2
This one is very similar in gameplay design to *League of Legends*, but it's a little bit more complicated to pick up. It has 110 playable heroes and even has a level editor to play around with!

SMITE
The gameplay here is similar to *LOL*'s, except for the over-the-shoulder perspective. The selection of gods comes from a wide range of cultures, meaning there are many characters to play as.

AWESOMENAUTS
Though it might look a little different, this 2-D game has many similarities to *LOL*. It's slightly easier and simpler to play, but it's a lot of fun all the same.

DID YOU KNOW?
Riot Games also releases info on champions who didn't make it past the concept stage, such as Gavid and Avasha!

FINAL FANTASY

THE LEGEND CONTINUES

It's the RPG series that has touched the hearts of everyone who has played it, thanks to its emotional and deep story lines, gorgeous design, and intricate gameplay.

Final Fantasy has long been one of the biggest series in gaming, and its fan base keeps growing, with the recent releases of *Final Fantasy X/X-2 HD* and *Final Fantasy Type-0 HD* bringing old classics to new gamers, plus cute spin-offs such as the musical *Theatrhythm Final Fantasy: Curtain Call* taking the games in a new direction.

But even with all that excitement, the main event is still to come, with the forthcoming *Final Fantasy XV* looking like yet another incredible experience that will take the famous series to a whole new level!

DID YOU KNOW?

Final Fantasy was going to be creator Hironobu Sakaguchi's last game (hence the name). Of course, it was a hit, so no retiring for him.

STATS

The highest rated in the series (according to Metacritic) is *Final Fantasy IX*, sitting on a lofty **94**

The lowest is *Final Fantasy: All the Bravest*, a touch-action RPG, with a **25**

The bestselling is *Final Fantasy VII*, with **10 million sales**

The original *Final Fantasy* is available on **8 different platforms**

There have been **110 million sales** worldwide since 1987, and it's the eighth bestselling game franchise of all time

TOP 5 CHARACTERS

BARRETT (FINAL FANTASY VII)

1 Barrett is Mr. T with bad language and a Gatling gun on his arm. He made a huge impression on gamers when he burst onto the scene, insulting grumpy old Cloud Strife.

LAGUNA LOIRE (FINAL FANTASY VIII)

2 Squall Leonheart may have been the cover star and had a pretty cool weapon, but Laguna was more fun and much less mopey.

KEFKA (FINAL FANTASY VI)

3 Kefka is a bad guy so horrible and remorseless, he makes Sephiroth look like Dumbledore. He just really enjoys making people's lives miserable. Plus, he's a clown. Clowns are the worst.

DID YOU KNOW?

Fantasy VII was originally going [to be] made for the Super Nintendo [an]d was going to take place in modern-day New York.

VINCENT VALENTINE (FINAL FANTASY VII)

4 The coolest good guy in *FFVII*, he was like a vampire version of Batman. He got his own game, too.

LULU (FINAL FANTASY X)

5 *Final Fantasy* has had some annoying people in it, so Lulu's no-nonsense, serious approach was refreshing. Her extravagant fashion sense (and the subsequent cosplaying) also helped.

HOW TO UNLOCK YUFFIE IN FINAL FANTASY VII!

Yuffie's a tricky ninja, and well worth getting along for the ride. In order to obtain her, you must first go to the Mythril Mines, then to any forest in the world.

You'll eventually get into a fight with Yuffie. She's fairly easy to beat, so don't panic. This isn't like fighting Emerald Weapon when you're only five hours into the game or something.

After beating her, you'll have a chat. Make sure you choose the following dialogue options: not interested, petrified, wait a second, that's right, let's hurry on.

Once you've completed the above steps, Yuffie will chase after you to join the party, and you'll have a new friend! Replace one of your current party members with Yuffie and you can start using her in battle.

FINAL FANTASY

PAOLO ZAROTTI

WHY? Huge collection . . . tattoos . . . a son named Zack.

HOW? Like many, Paolo got into the franchise through *Final Fantasy VII*. He didn't stop there, though, and his love burgeoned into wonderful obsession. He has multiple copies of all the games and numerous tattoos, and he even named his son Zack after the *Final Fantasy VII* character. It's a cool name—not as cool as Turok, but still pretty good.

COMMENT

Lydia Ellery
Squidgaming and
Ginx TV presenter

For me, *Final Fantasy* signifies a very specific time in my life. The glory PS1 days of *VII*, *VIII*, and *IX* were obsessions of mine as a preteen, and when real life got to be too much, I would hide in their fantastical adventures and beautiful worlds. I loved the days of text dialogue when I could make up the characters' voices myself. Whether I was dealing with insecurities and facing the hardest foe with Cloud, struggling with love and responsibilities as Squall, or asking the deep questions with Vivi, they were constant companions to me, and I look back on those memories fondly.

DID YOU KNOW?

The movie *Final Fantasy: The Spirits Within* lost $120 million at the box office, making it the second-biggest animated flop of all time. Oops.

DID YOU KNOW?

Designer Tetsuya Nomura considered turning the upcoming *FFXV* into a musical. He's now working on *Kingdom Hearts III*.

TIME LINE

1987 – FINAL FANTASY
1988 – FINAL FANTASY II
1990 – FINAL FANTASY III
1991 – FINAL FANTASY IV
1992 – FINAL FANTASY V
1994 – FINAL FANTASY VI
1997 – FINAL FANTASY VII
1999 – FINAL FANTASY VIII
2000 – FINAL FANTASY IX
2001 – FINAL FANTASY X
2002 – FINAL FANTASY XI
2003 – FINAL FANTASY X-2
2006 – FINAL FANTASY XII
2009 – FINAL FANTASY XIII
2010 – FINAL FANTASY XIV
2011 – FINAL FANTASY XIII-2
2013 – LIGHTNING RETURNS: FINAL FANTASY XIII
2013 – FINAL FANTASY XIV: A REALM REBORN

ALSO CHECK OUT . . .

LOST ODYSSEY

From *Final Fantasy* creator Hironobu Sakaguchi, this is a *Final Fantasy* game in all but name. It's also utterly heartbreaking, and guaranteed to have even the hardest among you fighting back the tears.

KINGDOM HEARTS

What do you get if you cross *Final Fantasy* with Disney? No, it's not Goofy with an anime hairdo, it's *Kingdom Hearts*! *Final Fantasy* characters clash with Disney ones in not-so-mortal combat. It's all very cute and colorful.

XENOBLADE CHRONICLES

It may look a bit dated, but this Japanese RPG offers enormous scale, plenty of quests, and a main character with a massive sword, so it crosses off a lot of things on the *Final Fantasy* checklist. It's getting a rerelease on the new 3DS soon, and a sequel. Hooray!

THE LEGEND OF ZELDA

USE THE TRIFORCE!

Zelda is one of those series that does everything with almost dizzying perfection: There's meaty combat, an engaging story line, larger-than-life enemies, and fantastically puzzling puzzles. With the recent releases of *Ocarina of Time* and *Majora's Mask* on 3DS, along with the upcoming *The Legend of Zelda 2016*, more players than ever before are discovering Nintendo's famous series.

The games center on Link, a hero of few words who lets his Master Sword do his talking. He's often tasked with rescuing Princess Zelda from Ganon, a mission that takes him all over the whimsical world of Hyrule, a land stuffed with luscious landscapes, wacky townsfolk, and rich lore. No wonder players keep coming back for more . . .

STATS

The original *Legend of Zelda* game sold over **6 million copies**

The only *Zelda* game to have beaten those sales since is *Twilight Princess*, which sold over **8 million copies**

The games consistently generate impressive scores on Metacritic, the highest of which was *The Wind Waker*'s **96**

The *Legend of Zelda* series has sold over **69 million units**

A **13**-episode animated series, *The Legend of Zelda*, aired in 1989

There have been **17** official *Zelda* games

TOP **5** BOSS FIGHTS

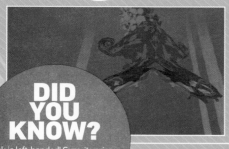

MOLGERA (THE WIND WAKER)

1 As if *Zelda* bosses aren't hard enough already, to beat Molgera, the boss of the Wind Temple, you need to get close to his weak spot—his tongue—to cause any damage. Careful he doesn't eat you, and watch out for the Molgera larvae!

DID YOU KNOW?

Link is left-handed! Sure, it varies a bit from game to game, but in most he'll hold his Master Sword aloft with his left hand!

DARK LINK (THE ADVENTURE OF LINK)

2 What a twist! Who'd have thought that you'd have to defeat your own doppelganger when you stepped into that final boss arena? Dark Link makes for a very difficult—and notorious—foe!

GANON (A LINK TO THE PAST)

3 You knew this wasn't going to be easy. He's appeared in numerous end-of-game arenas, but Ganon's ability to warp and shoot fireballs makes him particularly tough in *A Link to the Past*!

GYORG (MAJORA'S MASK)

4 Even when he's struck, this guy doesn't stay down long enough for Link to get in there and cause much damage, which makes your ability to react and respond to the situation quickly crucial to winning this battle. Don't get dragged underwater!

TWINROVA (OCARINA OF TIME)

5 The twin witches from *Ocarina of Time*, recently released again on 3DS, are able to individually target Link, cursing him with fire and ice spells. Link has to use their powers against them!

TOP TIPS FOR THE LEGEND OF ZELDA: MAJORA'S MASK 3D!

GET MORE RUPEES

In the south Termina Field, near Milk Road, you'll find a huge bird that steals rupees. If you attack and kill it, it will leave behind a golden rupee! You can repeat this as often as you need to.

ADVANCE TIME

To move the in-game clock from day to night (or vice versa), play this tune on the Ocarina: C-Right(2), A(2), C-Down(2). If it's evening, it'll switch to 6 AM; if it's early, it'll become 6 PM!

INCREASE YOUR QUIVER SIZE

To upgrade the Large Quiver to carry 40 arrows, you'll need to score 40 or more at the Town Shooting Gallery. To get the largest quiver—which holds 50 arrows—get a perfect score!

HOLD 500 RUPEES!

Is your wallet too small to carry all of Link's money? Find all the Gold Skulltula Tokens hidden in the Oceanside Spider House and you'll increase your wallet to hold 500 rupees!

MEET THE SUPERFAN

ELLIE SPANOVIC

WHY? The magic of Nintendo drew Ellie in . . . and now she's a huge collector!

HOW? Ellie totally fell in love with the world of Hyrule as a teenager. All the puzzles, dungeons, and amazing environments in the games make it her favorite series of all time—she doesn't think she'll ever stop loving it! Here are just a few of her favorite and most treasured *Zelda* goodies. With *The Legend of Zelda* on Wii U still to come, you can be sure that Ellie will soon have plenty more *Zelda* merchandise to add to her collection!

CHECK OUT . . .

THE WIND WAKER HD,
Wii U (2013)

Our own favorite *Zelda* adventure is *The Legend of Zelda: The Wind Waker,* which was released for Nintendo's much-loved GameCube back in 2002. What if you missed out, though? Fortunately, it's been remastered in sparkling HD for Wii U, so you can experience the stunning cel-shaded art style at its absolute best while also enjoying the delightful and timeless mix of sailing, adventuring, and puzzling! You can even take selfies in *The Wind Waker HD,* an addition that's way more fun than you might have thought . . .

DID YOU KNOW?
WWE wrestler Cody Rhodes has Triforce symbols on his boots—he's a big fan of the series and replays his favorites every year!

DID YOU KNOW?

Zelda creator Shigeru Miyamoto was inspired by the wife of *Great Gatsby* author F. Scott Fitzgerald— her first name was Zelda!

TIME LINE

1986	THE LEGEND OF ZELDA
1987	THE ADVENTURE OF LINK
1991	A LINK TO THE PAST
1993	THE LEGEND OF ZELDA: LINK'S AWAKENING
1998	THE LEGEND OF ZELDA: OCARINA OF TIME
2000	THE LEGEND OF ZELDA: MAJORA'S MASK
2001	ORACLE OF AGES / ORACLE OF SEASONS
2002	A LINK TO THE PAST / FOUR SWORDS / THE WIND WAKER
2004	FOUR SWORDS ADVENTURES: THE MINISH CAP
2006	TWILIGHT PRINCESS
2007	PHANTOM HOURGLASS
2009	SPIRIT TRACKS
2011	SKYWARD SWORD
2013	A LINK BETWEEN WORLDS
2015	THE LEGEND OF ZELDA 2015

ALSO CHECK OUT . . .

3D DOT GAME HEROES

If the original *Legend of Zelda* game had been made for the PS3, it might have looked a bit like this! The kingdom was once a 2-D, pixelated world, but the King decreed that the kingdom make the switch to 3-D.

OKAMI

As white wolf Amaterasu, you must travel around the world, battling enemies and helping townsfolk. Sound familiar? Capcom's classic was given a high-def makeover. Check out the unique Celestial Brush, too!

BASTION

A different but enjoyable take on the RPG adventure game, with one of the most ear-tickling soundtracks you'll ever have the pleasure of hearing. Bonus points for the wonderful narration, too!

LEGO GAMES

What do you get when you combine some of your favorite movies with one of your favorite toys? A whole host of *LEGO* games, in which you can build planes as Indiana Jones, create spells with Harry Potter, and save New York City with Iron Man and the gang.

After visiting the bricktastic versions of Hogwarts and Middle-earth, among others, where else can we go? Jurassic Park, of course! *LEGO Jurassic World* will cover all the films in the series, from the groundbreaking original to the brand-new *Jurassic World*. There are over 100 characters to unlock, and yes, you get to play as the dinosaurs, too!

Perfect timing, too, since Batman fans will have just finished up the DLC for *LEGO Batman 3: Beyond Gotham* . . .

DID YOU KNOW?

The first *LEGO* game to be released was *LEGO Island*, a PC game that let you explore, interact, and even design your own vehicles!

STATS

So far,

55

LEGO games have been released

4

billion studs is the limit in *LEGO Batman: The Videogame*

There are

155

playable characters in *LEGO Marvel Super Heroes*

There are

3.13

million sales, on average, of each release